Best Spiritual Literature

Best Spiritual Literature

Vol. 7

2022

Edited by Luke Hankins, Nathan Poole, & Karen Tucker

ORISON BOOKS

ISSN: 2833-1168
ISBN 978-1-949039-37-5

Orison Books
PO Box 8385
Asheville, NC 28814
www.orisonbooks.com

Distributed to the trade by Itasca Books
952-223-8373 / orders@itascabooks.com
www.itascabooks.com

Best Spiritual Literature is cataloged in the EBSCO*host* digital database.

Cover photo by Pawel Czerwinski. Used courtesy of Unsplash.

Manufactured in the U.S.A.

CONTENTS

ABOUT BEST SPIRITUAL LITERATURE

Best Spiritual Literature is the new name of *The Orison Anthology* (ISSN 2380-7776), which was published for six years under the original name. *Best Spiritual Literature*, under the same editorship and publisher, continues the same mission to collect the finest spiritually engaged writing that appeared in periodicals in the preceding year. Thus, this inaugural volume bearing the new name is numbered 7.

In addition to reprinted material, each year the anthology also includes new, previously unpublished works of fiction, nonfiction, and poetry by the winners of The *Best Spiritual Literature* Awards.

Ser Álida

Love thy neighbor.

1 Peter 4:8

> *Above all, love each other deeply, because love covers over a multitude of sins.*

The first time I ate pussy, I was ten, maybe eleven. Esmeralda, la gordita del 3B.

Her family moved into our building in Villa Faro early summer '98 on the floor right above ours. Life was simple. I worried about simple things: picking up before Mami got home, not missing *La Mentira*, wondering when my titties would start poking out or why my pubic hair was growing in patches. Then, she pulled up. Andaban en un camioncito azul, a single cabin '87 Toyota pickup. Como el de los plataneros, but filled with their lives instead. She struggled off the truck juggling an oversized backpack stuffed full, a volleyball, a thick bible-looking book, and a white cat to her hip holding on for dear life.

Santo Domingo's skies were stripped of clouds. Ella parecía de porcelana: tall, thick, paled to paper. The sun bounced off her cheeks tinting them pink, and she squinted away, the light unwelcomed. Mamá Tina and I played bríca on the front lot, hiding from the sun under a flamboyán. Ni saludarón. They moved quickly, quietly, not interrupting the afternoon, and they lived in the same way, careful not to move the trappings before them. From our post, we watched them unload what little they brought: a stand alone fan, two mattresses, a small round table, two chairs, a television and a few taped up boxes. Her family was small. Three—well four, if you count Dionisio, their cat, mi pana from the jump, blinking a curious glare in my direction before the gate closed behind them.

"Pero ven acá Camila!?" Mamá Tina's voice shook me from across the table.

"I'm about to Mamá," I said, "don't rush me," but I kept daydreaming.

"Tu ve, that's why I can't play with you. Tira cualquier vaina ahí," she said before taking a long pull from her Marlboro Red, closing her eyes a moment then blowing the smoke at me. I breathed it in and chose my play.

Esmeralda and her folks made a few trips to unload the truck. She twirled across the parking lot right past us, and I followed the sound of her flip flops echoing through the gate, down the hall, up the stairs, past my floor, to the last door on the right. Mamá Yaya took the game. I shuffled the deck.

The summer moved unbothered. I kept count of her every move at a distance; learning her routines and chasing the echo of her body breaking through the walls that divided us. From my bedroom window I could hear the novelas on her tv, her broken laughter, the volleyball bouncing from her bedroom wall, her stomping feet chasing after Dionisio. I'd imagine knocking on her door and joining her and Dionisio on their laps around the living room, but I never mustered the courage. Instead, I started plotting ways of casually bumping into her; camping out in the parking lot in case she ever came out, following her to el colmado when she did, and making sure I could pull off at least half a smile whenever we made eye contact. I was curious, hungry, swimming in a newness so present and so hurried, I struggled to find balance. When you're eleven, love lacks frames of understanding or concrete definitions. I was falling though, right before her.

Eran testigos: Kingdom Hall on Sundays, Wednesday bible studies, Friday group prayers; no birthdays, no Christmas, no music. At most, Esmeralda sang hymns in the bathroom, and I listened embelesá, wanting things I'd yet to recognize. Mi familia wasn't particularly holy, Catholic by default. Mami tucked me in every night with a Padre Nuestro and two Ave Marias, but we only went to church if the holy ghost called us by name: weddings, baptisms, first communions, and a funeral here and there. Enough to keep a safe distance from the gates of hell, but not quite to avoid its parting flames. Faith escaped me. I chased it all summer bouncing from hallway to hallway after Esmeralda. If I had to believe in anything, her big ole brown eyes round like pebbles and the thick ass eyebrows above them sent me to pray. I waited, filled with the hope only first times can give.

By September, Mami and Marcela, Esmeralda's mom, had become friends: cafecitos por la tarde, mercado runs, a favor here, another there.

"Vecina, ¿me cuida la niña por una horita?" Marcela asked Mami to keep an eye on Esmeralda every Wednesday during bible study.

"Cami, take some habichuelas to Marcela for a little taste." Mami would send me over every time she made something she was proud of.

"¡Vecina, la ropa—va a llover!" they'd yerp out a weather warning through the service window.

They bonded over the loneliness of motherhood. Mami was still bitter about Papi's bitch-ass exit and Marcela was weighed down by a husband who was there, but had stopped seeing her. They found solace in each other. They'd trade chismes about other neighbors and had long conversations about paradise and the afterlife. Mami stared blankly, gliding between Marcela's words always flooded with such enamouring conviction. Yet, Mami's faith bordered the well. She leaned over the edge sometimes, but never leapt in.

"Camila, you're going with Marcela to Kingdom Hall on Wednesday," she'd tell me every so often after chatting with Marcela, trying to get me on the path to sanctification. Their talks always shook Mami's faith. She never visited Kingdom Hall or gave up on the Pope, but she always came back weary of salvation and took measurements—however minimal—to keep us saved.

School started de un día pa otro. Esmeralda went to La Gregorio Luperón, a public school in our neighborhood. I knew because some days we'd drive by her on our way to my school, swaying in her khaki skirt and tucked-in button up. She caught a motoconcho on the corner of La San Vicente with the rest of the neighborhood kids. Every time we'd drive by, Mami would warn me I'd be joining them soon, if Papi didn't come out his pocket with child support. Mami was still paying for El Victor Manuel on the other side of the city. She was struggling though. The school secretary would hand me the notices to take home at least once a week.

I started bumping into Esmeralda in the emergency staircase after school, but she never said anything beyond a hello and a smile. Neither did I. One afternoon I was feeling brave and brought her un frío frío de limón.

"You like frio frio?" I asked her.

"Claro." She looked back on her way up the stairs. "Ese es pa mi?"

"If you want it," I responded.

"Call me Nani," she told me, "that's what my friends call me."

"So we're friends in real life?" I asked jokingly.

"Maybe." She giggled in a way that made my throat tickle.

"I'm Camila, Cami for short," I mumbled nervously, never making eye contact.

"Camila José," she said confidently.

"Waitaminute—how you know?" I was surprised.

"Doña Yaya yells it out the window enough for the whole residencial to know." She wasn't lying.

"You can sing," the words streamed out of my chest after

weeks of faithful audience.

"You heard me?" she asked, raising her left eyebrow firmly my way.

I didn't want her to know that I'd been listening; laying on my back staring at the ceiling imagining her octave breaking through me. I pulled back embarrassed, leaning my shoulder against the hallway wall. She smiled and leaned in. She knew I'd been listening then, but what's worse, I knew she knew.

We met on the emergency staircase every afternoon, talked about all and nothing, played with Dionisio, she'd warn me about seventh grade, I'd complain about fifth. She liked bows on her hair and wore them all the time shifting between a scruffy side ponytail and two wavy pigtails on each side of her ears. I hated brushing my hair. My kinks fought against any disruption to their freeform. I rarely fought back.

Nani liked playing with my earlobe. She'd sit beside me, move my hair out of the way, and rub on my ear as she talked about her day. Her fingers whispered softly, dozing me out. No one, aside from Mamá Yaya, ever touched me so gently. Everything grew in such a way, calmly, uninterrupted, lust unceasingly bursting inside me, against my will or ability to recognize it: *Prepubescent Wet Dreams: A True Story*.

Le enseñé a jugar bríca y yax. She learned fast and soon started beating me every time. She tried, unsuccessfully, to get me jumping rope, but my lungs weren't cut out. I was clumsy, chubby, and too worried about breaking a sweat in front of her. I didn't learn, but we had fun trying. Our days turned to months like run-on sentences, no punctuation, playdates, weekends in el campo with Mamá Yaya, infinite late night chatters breaking through the crickets' harmony. I kept falling.

One day after school I saw her cutting through the parking lot hand in hand with Miguelito, el negrito del 5C. I watched from the balcony as they giggled and fiddled their way into the building, losing them at the entrance where my eyes could no longer reach. That afternoon she told me, hyped as fuck, that Miguelito asked her out, but she was "thinking about it, you know, you can't make it too easy on 'em." Pero, ¿y cuándo fue eso? Where was I? I panicked.

I was angry, but the sadness was more. If I had a chance, it ended with Miguelito. More words stumbled eagerly between her teeth. I heard nothing. The "us" I had sheltered myself behind undid itself before me. She, on the other hand, was happy, painfully so.

"Should I tell Mami? ¿Tu cree que se quille?" she asked excitedly.

I shrugged. She kept talking. I faded away.

It took me a minute, but I pretended shit was cool. I told her I was sick and skipped the staircase for a couple days. At the time, I wasn't too sure where the ache came from or if the feeling of loss had any real meaning.

Days later we met again and sat beside each other on the steps. Dionisio had gotten shots and laid his body heavily on Nani's side. She smelled like oatmeal. I, to be honest, was on the much mustier side. El sol aun estaba picando, bared of clouds to break its path. Our thighs glued together in sweaty patches of heat, we didn't move though, laughing and froclicking with one another. My neck melted into a stream down my chest where my shirt started to stick. She played with my bead bracelet, I wrote on her knee cap, namelessly building up.

Her eyes smiled at me like a dare, and my heartbeat raised to the top of my throat. And so we kissed. Well, I kissed her. She wanted me too, I think. I took the chance in a quiet moment. She stopped her eyes on mine with a grinning invitation, and I just, well, I kissed her. And she kissed me back for a few seconds; shut eye, wet, unsorted, naive, a question more than a kiss, a finding. I lived in her softness those few seconds, a home better than I'd imagined, a pathway. She breathed in between my breaths tickling my lips with her mustache. Home it was, pero que poco duró. She pulled away, and I watched her speed into the hallway. I sat at the top of the stairs unmoved wishing she'd look back at me. She didn't.

I waited faithfully, but Nani stopped coming out. I wanted to apologize, to take it all back, hold off on my move and maybe not move at all. We'd done something wrong. I'd done something wrong. I struggled to name what.

1 Corinthians 6:9-10

> *Or do you not know that wrongdoers will not inherit the kingdom of God? Do not be deceived: Neither the sexually immoral nor idolaters nor adulterers nor men who have sex with men nor thieves nor the greedy nor*

drunkards nor slanderers nor swindlers will inherit the kingdom of God.

And what if I kissed a girl?

Mami used to say I was different. Hollow, ain't it? I wonder what she meant. As I grew into myself, I started unthreading. Slowly, but steadily, coming undone. I told no one about Esmeralda. I knew not to. In Villa Faro, lesbianism was an invisible monster, hidden carefully away from the innocent eye. Our novelas weren't about Marias holding hands. Our love stories never had Cleo and Ursula kissing against the hood of a car. So what then set off this unquenchable fire? Villa Faro was all I'd known.

In Mami's house, gayness always followed an explanation, "Your tío Julio was like that, good peoples, but he died of AIDS," or, "Hardworking, pero maricón, you know? Que Dios lo tenga en su gloria!" I had no explanation. Nothing yet to shape these feelings. No clear articulation of who or what I was just a moment ago between Nani's lips.

I sought mirrors outside myself and bumped into a collective erasure, doubtful I even existed. Loneliness is a strong bitter when you can't find yourself outside yourself. Loneliness is a deep river when you're eleven; your toes wiggle at the surface not finding the bottom.

Un domingo, after weeks of silence, Nani came down to get me.

"¿Vamo pa' mi casa?" she invited me.

I can't remember if I answered, but I followed her down

the hall, up the stairs and into their apartment. We were alone. She skipped Kingdom Hall that morning. I overheard Marcela ask Mami to keep an eye on Nani. Something about "a lice breakout at bible camp" and "Nani staying home to be on the safe side."

"Ta to, what we about to do?" I stood at her door unmoved, a bit nervous and more so confused.

"¡Camina, ven!" She pulled me through the living room, past the bathroom and into her bedroom. *Yo Amo a Paquita Gallego* was on. "Vamo' a ver la novela," she told me.

Her room was bright, airy. The sun creeped through her curtains painting the walls. La magia de siempre, except the newness of our first kiss drowning every thought, every move, taking up space, closing us in. Dionisio laid on the bed. We sat facing each other on the floor, our palms pressed together as if in prayer. Y ahí hicimos misa.

I can't be sure where we began. Her leg extended over mine, she smiled, I smiled, I leaned in for a tap, she laid one on me. Her hands rushed unsettled all around my body, under my shirt, on my back, on my neck, behind my head, inside my shorts. I worried—about the hair patches, my flat chest, the heat rushing down my thighs (sweat, lust, both), about Mami downstairs, about Miguelito el del 5C, about Peter and Corinthians. I worried. I prayed. She kissed me.

Her fingers pressed against my crotch motioning in circles left and right. My clit swelled against them through the panties and shorts, growing into the novelty of the moment. My knees locked and my breath thickened—

angsty, confused, not understanding my body or my desires. I followed her lead, shaking in her hands y baboseandole la cara. Time echoed slowly around us. Soon we were naked from the bottom down. Her toto wasn't like mine. Su toto no tenía frente, no mountain to climb. I didn't have to search for her parts, they rose to the surface. Nani's pubic hair was long and fine, perfectly covering her lips. She grabbed my hand and pressed it against her clit, mimicking what she'd done on mine a moment before. Her wetness leaked between my fingers, gluing them together while also helping them glide.

"¿Qué hago?" I asked, my nervous stare meeting her before my words.

"Kiss it," she said through a soft smirk.

I was scared. Once, in Mami's room, I played a video she'd forgotten on the VHS. It was less than three minutes before I got caught, but it was three minutes too long. A lady laid on the couch wide-legged, and a man kneeled in front of her. He fingered her toto hardcore and French kissed it between pumps. Felicia, la trabajadora, walked in on me and told Mami. I was grounded for the rest of the summer. I hated the stupid video until this moment. ¿Qué sabía yo que los totos eran para mamarse? Nani laid in front of me wide-legged too, her pubic hair visibly damped, her breaths rushed twice as mine, waiting for me to do something, anything. And so, I did. I leeched my lips on her clit and kissed it, slobbering on my chest and gripping on to her thighs. The floor helped cool our bodies. La novela drowned her grasps for air.

I was stuck on Nani when Marcela opened the door. She found us on the floor naked, Nani spilling from the edges of my mouth, her panties wrapped around her ankle, mine somewhere on the floor. She pulled Nani by the elbow, y a mí ni me miró. I picked up what I could and ran my ass home. Dignity escaped me. Fermín, her dad, stood at the door waiting for me to get out. I did, head down, y sin mucho ruido.

2 Peter 3:17

> *You therefore, beloved, knowing this beforehand, be on your guard so that you are not carried away by the error of unprincipled men and fall from your own steadfastness*

.

I rushed into the shower unnoticed. Mami was asleep on the couch. For the next hour, I scrubbed Nani off my body: every look, every smile, every touch, every sweat patch, su olorcito a avena, all the desires that rested on my belly. I prayed all night; if only I didn't look at her, if only she didn't look back. I prayed all night; that Marcela wouldn't tell Mami and that she didn't whip Nani too hard. I prayed all night; as if praying hard enough would turn back time, bring me to a beginning where Nani wasn't. I prayed all night; and found no prayer to rid my body of this sin, to help reconcile the feelings of joy and shame that danced inside me.

Nani went ghost for the next couple of weeks. There were no hymns flying out of her bathroom window, no novelas sounding off her television, and no stomping feet on her floors. I saw her a few times at the motoconcho stop with Miguelito and them, but she never came back to the emergency staircase again.

They moved out the following summer, loading their little pickup as quietly as they came. I watched them from the balcony. Cogieron to'a La San Vicente. She sat between Marcela and Fermín, squashed inside the one cabin. I watched until they disappeared, herded through the evening's traffic. Parecían hormiguitas mientras se me escapaban.

Originally published in Southern Humanities Review

Jai Hamid Bashir

The Apiarists

No one wants to go back
home after ascending all this way
with lost rent. This season we want to be apiarists.

Corrugated in palm folds, the rope of your courage
carries me to jump into the reservoir
from the yarded grass of afternight.

We humble queens and sugar for our hunger.
Listen, a godsong is in the bees.
Bereft wind—soft as an animal.

A dog steadies his head in rain. Artful eyes search shivers
    of sky.
You take photographs. Nectar arrives
from the Ancient Greek for *death* and *overcome*.

Practice, you said after we were followed
by a stinging congregation that doesn't practice
death and mercy on the same meter.

Underwater, in an unsacred baptism, I held
my breath and counted until you drew us
back to nectar the surface. The swarm rose like a cloud.

My summery dress, my bare-lillied brown
skin with learned stings. Grid and another grid
of the most tender mob seduced by smoke.

In each photograph is what was not photographed.
In each language is what is not language.
In every godsong is what is not sung nor divine.

Originally published in The Tampa Review

Ellen Bass

During the Pandemic I Listen to the July 26, 1965, Juan-les-Pins Recording of *A Love Supreme*

The first familiar, know-them-anywhere notes bless me
this savage morning. Coltrane's horn racing
up and down every alley, in and out of veins and over the faces
of lakes and into the heart of stones.
And when he repeats *A love supreme* again and again,
it's as though, if he says it enough, he can ease
that mercy down into me, into the tiny ossicular chain,
the chemical rush, the spark, and my brain
getting it—if even just
for this thirty-two minutes and forty-eight seconds.
My daughter's been sick seven weeks with the virus.
Yesterday she felt a little bored, she texted. And I grab that
like a shopping cart. I load it up with hope.
Make it prayer. When the day's portion of the Torah is recited,
someone stands by to correct mistakes.
The words must vibrate precisely in the air.
So I open my door
to the breath of his instrument
that refuses nothing, lavishing the grass, gutters and trees,
concrete, cars, the gopher pulling down the new lettuces.
This generous sound that can mean
anything, nothing, whatever you need.
And isn't that god? Isn't that it?
This shivering? This fall to my knees?
Gods do walk among us.
But humans are, after all, a broken promise.
And yet, these humans seem to be trying

to enter . . . what?
I can almost hear it. This old planet.
Worms passing earth through their tissue.
Orchids, corn, mockingbirds throwing themselves into song
like there's no tomorrow. Which there may not be.
Yet, still a mountain. Still wind.
And Coltrane still offering the same four notes
like a teacher who is infinitely patient.
He's telling me it's worth it
to be in a body. He's telling me
I'm alive in a beach town in California and my daughter
in a high rise in Vancouver, my girl,
lying feverish on the couch she's been lying on
forty-nine days and forty-nine nights, still alive.

Originally published in New England Review

Jack B. Bedell

Ghost Forest

—Manchac, after Frank Relle's photograph,
"Alhambra"

1.

Backlit by city and refinery's glow
these cypress bones shimmer

on the still lake's surface.
It's easy to see a storm's

coming with the sky rolling
gray overhead and the water

glass-calm. Even easier to know
these trees have weathered

some rough winds, their branches
here and there, pointing this

a-way and that at what
we've done to this place.

Their trunks gather here
like hoary, Old Testament prophets

come down from the mountain
to rest in this body dump,

gold light hitting the moss
        all Luminol-shine and whisper.

2.

Water's the only thing
        that gets in here easily, pushed

in by storms or poured
        through spillway gates.

Years of its salt have loosened
        the coast line's faith, turned

forest to roots and sawgrass,
        constant loss. This water

rises, seeps, leaves doubt
        everywhere dirt should be.

It's not worth lying down
        in the hull of your boat

to scrape under the rail trellis
        if you're only coming here

to see what used to be. Do it
        so you can hear the ghost forest

sing about what's coming next
        after the water's had its way.

3.

What is moss if it isn't
memory? It hangs off these branches,

sways on the breeze like Merton's
prayers, the closest these trees

will get to needles again. Everything else
here is dead still, waiting for the storm

to blow in. No frog bellow,
no heron flap—just moss

waving and the water's slow rise
to prove this place breathes.

Stillness is faith, locust's whine
benediction here, and this moss

knows all there is to know
about holding on, and air,

and how fully empty time is
with all this water aching

to fill it. Trunks. Branches.
Sky bruising into storm.

Originally published in Psaltery & Lyre

Wendy Cheng

The Instant You Entered the Black Hole

1.

Teh-chang came home a couple of days after the surgery, wheeled out of the hospital with a cotton bandage wrapped around his head cartoon-style and, even stranger-looking, a white mesh Styrofoam netting gathered into a point on top of that, which made him resemble a delicate fruit packaged for long-distance transportation.

He had survived having his skull sawn open, a surgeon slicing out a tumor over a centimeter and a half in diameter and then putting his head back together. If that were all, it would have been a happy ending. Instead, it was just the beginning.

The brain tumor was not the source but an emissary. *Stage 4 lung cancer.* The intern just happened to mention the words printed on the chart during his morning rounds. And that was how they found out.

A black hole is a place where the laws of physics as we know them break down. Einstein taught us that gravity warps space itself, causing it to curve. So given a dense enough object, space-time can become so warped that it twists in on itself, burrowing a hole

All italicized text about black holes is from Amanda Gefter's article "The Strange Fate of a Person Falling into a Black Hole," which appeared on BBC Earth's site in May 2015. Some excerpts are slightly altered from the original.

through the very fabric of reality.

The instant you entered the black hole, reality would split in two. In one, you would be instantly incinerated, and in the other you would plunge on into the black hole utterly unharmed.

Much later, his daughter found the article about black holes. When she read it, she felt a powerful longing. In this reality, he had died and become ash. She knew this to be true. She had been with him when he took his last breath and then stopped breathing forever. She had felt the warmth dissipate from his body over the course of several hours, until he was wrapped in a sheet and taken away. She had touched his ashes with her own hands and rolled tiny fragments of his bones between her fingers.

But what if, as the physicists hypothesize, the universe split?

"There will be many things to happen," he had written to her in an email during the weeks after the surgery. "Just be quiet and wait and see. I will be all right."

As you go deeper into the black hole, space becomes ever more curvy until, at the centre, it becomes infinitely curved. This is the singularity. Space and time cease to be meaningful ideas, and the laws of physics as we know them—all of which require space and time—no longer apply.

Immediately after the surgery, he was different. Usually reserved and silent to a fault (in his wife's opinion), he marveled out loud at how beautiful the nurse was, how incredibly handsome the surgeon. The nurse, a blonde-haired woman dressed all in pink, appeared to be a crew member on a spaceship, part of his abduction to another planet or galaxy. Crying, he asked his wife, "Can I be a writer?" More firmly, he said, "From now on, we only say positive things." Turning to his son, he observed, "You have big ears." His wife and daughter and son laughed through their tears.

What happens here, no one knows. Another universe? Oblivion? The back of a bookcase? It's a mystery.

Before he retired and started writing poetry full-time, he had been a nuclear physicist who studied fusion energy. He had a lifelong interest in theoretical physics, which led naturally to interests in philosophy, religion, and ancient history, and a belief in the likelihood of extraterrestrial life. After the surgery he became obsessed with "the issue of the universe. It is fundamental," as he wrote in an email to a scientist friend. Of his daughter, he asked insistently, with the manic energy that pulsed through him in those weeks, "Are you Heisenberg or are you Einstein?"

His daughter seemed confused.

He knew she didn't know anything about Werner Heisenberg, or even Albert Einstein. He wanted to tell her that this was a question concerning his own fate and, indeed, the fate of the universe. Heisenberg's uncertainty principle posited an underlying unknowability in the universe. In contrast, Einstein believed in an underlying order, that the complete predictability of physical laws determined the course of events. If Einstein was right, following the laws of classical physics, then the laws of the universe could not be altered; his illness would follow its inevitable course, and he would die. If Heisenberg was right, however, following the laws of quantum physics, there were other possibilities: unknown quantities, alternate universes, and multiple realities.

She had studied art and literature and didn't know anything about physics, though, so he didn't try to explain. Someday, probably soon, she would see for herself.

When you reach the horizon, you freeze, like someone has hit the pause button. You remain plastered there, motionless, stretched across the surface of the horizon as a growing heat begins to engulf you.

According to an outside viewer, you are slowly obliterated by the stretching of space, the stopping of time and the fires of Hawking radiation. Before you ever cross over into the black hole's darkness, you're reduced to ash.

But before we plan your funeral, let's view this gruesome scene from your point of view. Now, something even stranger happens: nothing.

In the wake of his surgery, his world changed. Everything he encountered was suffused with special significance, and every person could be conversed with. When hot-air balloons drifted close over the house near sunset, as they often did in the spring, taking off from a nearby open field, he ran out to wave to the passengers, still wearing his Styrofoam netting on his head. "They came to see me," he told his daughter, grinning happily. After each doctor's visit, he kept the hospital's paper identification bracelet on his wrist and thrust it at strangers, informing them enthusiastically, "I am a hospital patient, dying of lung cancer!"

You sail straight into nature's most ominous destination without so much as a bump or a jiggle—and certainly no stretching, slowing or scalding radiation. That's because you're in freefall, and therefore you feel no gravity.

After all, the event horizon is not like a brick wall floating in space. It's an artefact of perspective. An observer who remains outside the black hole can't see through it, but that's not your problem. As far as you're concerned there is no horizon.

Two weeks after the surgery, he ran away from home.

He had been posting increasingly candid messages on a family webpage his daughter had set up to share news and support during his treatment. He added his middle-of-the-night musings (he could not sleep at all) about his love, about the universe, about having to get up to pee—everything that came into his mind.

> S. may not be happy because she always
> thought I cared and care for others, and

> never care for her. I always ignore her. I always lied to her. I never loved her. But I want to tell all of you that I loved her, and love her. The only thing I don't really know is that whether I loved her before I was born. There is another thing even if she still not believe it, I will go to another world to find the answer whether I will love her there. My prediction is that I will. But you will have to wait, like S. She has to wait.

His wife and son were not happy.

He knew they were talking about deleting the page. They were going to cut off his access to the outside world. What choice did he have? He had to go. That afternoon he sent his son an email titled "My Last Email" and walked out of the house.

After an hour had passed and he hadn't come back, his wife went out in her car to look for him. She spotted him about a mile away, sitting on the steps of the library, but when he saw her, he ran.

His daughter was in New York, traveling for work, when she received a string of urgent calls and text messages from her brother. Had their father called her? He had not. Panicking, she dialed his cell phone number several times in a row, but it only rang and rang, and went to voice mail.

Back home, his wife and son decided to call the sheriff.

Because of Teh-chang's erratic state of mind and their location in a wealthy area, the police acted immediately, sending a helicopter to circle the typically quiet enclave. The helicopter shone a searchlight through the tall eucalyptus trees, over the gentle slopes of the golf course, onto the dirt paths by the large reservoir abutting the other side of their street, and over the ominously dark two-lane highway upon which cars and trucks sped recklessly into rocky, mountainous terrain. They used a loudspeaker to call for him, the foreign last name and the bright, sweeping lights perhaps striking fear into the hearts of their elderly white neighbors. The landscape yielded no answers.

By that time, he was far away.

Sure, if the black hole were smaller you'd have a problem. The force of gravity would be much stronger at your feet than at your head, stretching you out like a piece of spaghetti. But lucky for you this is a big one, millions of times more massive than our Sun, so the forces that might spaghettify you are feeble enough to be ignored.

In fact, in a big enough black hole, you could live out the rest of your life pretty normally.

2.

He walked out of the house that afternoon with no destination in mind. His thin rubber flip-flops made a slapping sound on the asphalt road. Every once in a while, a large SUV would barrel past him, crossing into the other lane to do so, but no one else was out. He himself had walked this road hundreds of times and had driven it every day over the past seventeen years. It was a golden spring afternoon, and the air smelled of orange blossoms and freshly cut grass. When he got to the main road, he didn't keep his head down, as he would have before (his previous self would have been contemplating something and also wanting to avoid any attention from the local security patrol, who tended to stop single men with brownish skin). Instead he tilted his face upward toward the sky and grinned. It was a beautiful world. Why hadn't he always known that? Why didn't *they* know that?

As he walked down the pedestrian path parallel to the road, he was flanked by the rolling hills of the golf course on the left and immaculately maintained bushes of blooming flowers and fragrant herbs on his right. He could hear the deep metallic *tink* of golf club smacking golf ball every now and then, imagined in his mind the tiny pitted globes hurtling high into the air.

When he got to the bridge, he looked for the egret, as he always did—that majestic, pristinely white creature of infinite patience—but it was not there. Instead, there were two boys, sandy haired and serious faced. They crouched halfway down the bank, staring longingly toward a soccer ball, which floated rather unmovingly on a thick scrim of algae, close to where the small creek either began or ended in the circular mouth of a large concrete storm drain.

He thought about how his own kids had passed over this wooden bridge every day when they were little, walking home from elementary school. For a period of time, the boy had caught crayfish here and taken them home to live in the square fountain by the swimming pool. (The adults had thought about cooking them to eat, but the kids only wanted to keep them as pets and feed *them*, watching as the creatures snatched silver guppies midcurrent with their surprisingly quick claws and then used those same claws to stuff the soft iridescent flesh into their tiny crustacean maws.) These kids, he realized, were just like his kids, before his kids grew up into reticent and rather joyless adults.

"Need help?" he called, his voice cracking only slightly. (He was not used to speaking loudly, had been doing so only these past couple of weeks, since his world had broken open into these luminous spaces of beauty and possibility.)

The boys seemed surprised but only for a moment. "Yeah," one of them nodded. "We're trying to get our ball."

It was not difficult to ease himself down the bank and wade into the water. It was, however, deeper than he expected, and colder. He was up to his waist, the algae clinging to his wet shirt, by the time he reached the ball. With both hands, he grasped the ball carefully and held it up in front of his chest all the way back to the bank.

"Thanks!" both boys yelped when he handed it back to them, thrilled by this unexpected turn of events. They were not yet old enough to be frightened or upset by the sight of a grown man fully dressed and half-soaked with creek water.

"No problem!" He smiled. He felt like singing. It had been such an easy thing to do for them. It was not how it was at home. His family was so hard to help. To his wife, everything he did was wrong. And now he had gotten cancer and would be such a burden on her. *A failure of a man*, his earlier self intoned. But he pushed the thought away. Now, there was only this day, this afternoon, these boys, this victory. He could do anything.

When he got to town, he sat down on the brick steps of the library to rest. He had been there just a few minutes when suddenly his wife pulled up to the curb in her white Mercedes. Through the tinted windows, he could see her mouth set in a grim line. Oh no, he wasn't going back to that. He ran.

It was not hard to duck behind the low buildings, to slip away between them. He walked quickly through a courtyard, passed a stodgy restaurant they had gone to a few times when the kids were young, a real-estate office, a law firm. Without really thinking about it, he found himself standing in front of a plain white building that said First Church of Christ, Scientist. Christ, Scientist! Grinning, he walked up to the double doors and pulled on the handle. It was locked. He frowned. Weren't places of God supposed to be open all the time? He could see a young woman sitting behind a desk inside. He knocked on the window. She looked up but didn't move. What was wrong with her? Didn't she understand that the door should not be locked? Impatient, he knocked on the glass harder, with an open hand. Now he saw fear on her face. She stood up, but instead of coming toward the door, she went the other direction and disappeared from sight. He waited. He banged on the glass again, but no one came.

Never mind. He knew there was another church down the road. Maybe there would be some true Christians there.

The doors were not locked. He found himself inside an auditorium. There was a rehearsal of some kind going on. Several young people were speaking loudly and making sweeping gestures with their hands. He smiled at them, and they smiled back, without fear or suspicion. This was how a church should be, he thought.

After the rehearsal was over, he approached one of them, a young man with a particularly kind face. It was not hard to persuade the man to give him a ride. As strange as Teh-chang looked (his pants were still a bit damp), wasn't he like Jesus, a humble, wandering prophet? He was not Christian himself, but he had always known Christians and been interested in Christianity. Christians understood that there was something much bigger than human beings in the universe. And they believed in life after death.

The young man was driving back to his home in Temecula, about forty miles away. Teh-chang knew then where he needed to go. At first, he had told the young man he could drop him off in Temecula, but as they approached the turnoff for the place he really wanted, he told him plainly, "Turn here."

"I can't." For the first time, the young man, really just a boy compared to Teh-chang, looked frightened. "I, uh, have a date tonight. I can't be late."

"She'll be impressed!" Teh-chang insisted. "You helped a stranger in need. It's very Christian. I will even help you score points on the date."

Finally, reluctantly, the young man made the turn. But after that, he focused only on driving and didn't want to talk anymore. That was fine. Teh-chang's destination, the one he now realized had been in the back of his mind all along, was close at hand.

He felt so powerful. He had walked out of his house with nothing but the clothes he was wearing, his wallet, and his cell phone. Without calling anyone or spending any money, he had bent the universe to his will. Strangers were so kindhearted, so easily manipulated. It was remarkable that he had never realized his own capability.

He knew he had had to leave his family to come into it, this power. They wanted to censor him, to isolate him. They didn't understand him, had never understood him. He did not hate them—no, of course not—they were his angels, he had always loved them, maybe even before he knew them. But they seemed very far away now, and that was a good thing.

3.

Looking back now, his daughter realizes they should have known exactly where to find him. He had written it plainly himself, after all, in that "last email" he sent to his son: "I long to play slot machines until the day I die."

Pala Casino sat in the San Luis Rey River valley, in remote northern inland San Diego County. In the spring it was a wistfully beautiful place. The valley's eponymous river, dry for much of the year, asserted itself, greening the trees and attracting songbirds to its rocky creekbeds. Graceful cottonwood trees reached their intricately twisting branches up into the air, and their heart-shaped leaves fluttered in the breeze. They released wispy puffs of cotton that drifted in the air like fairy dust.

And then there was the casino, which rose out of the dry land like a magical castle.

This was the land and casino of the Pala Band of Mission Indians, whose Luiseño and Kuupangaxwichem (or Cupeño) ancestors lived and worked and thrived in the region for thousands of years, and then suffered and were forced together here, under first the Spanish mission system and later the American reservation system. Some of them still lived here today, in double-wide trailers and modest ranch homes that lay just past the shadow of the casino.

But Teh-chang didn't know about any of that; like most of the people who came to this flashy temple of dreams, he didn't even think to wonder about it. On that day, in the passenger seat of the silently afraid Christian boy who drove where he was told, he just followed his heart, and his heart wanted to play slot machines.

Years ago, when he had gone to the Casino by himself for

the first time, he felt a sense of freedom he rarely had before. No one in his family knew he was there. His kids had their own lives, and across the ocean in Taiwan, where his wife had moved back for work, it was the middle of the night and his wife was sleeping.

He loved the utter chance of the slot machines, their colorful graphics, the thrill of possibility, the repetition of pressing the buttons and watching the images spin again and again. It didn't matter if he won; all he had to do was not lose too much. It was unlike anything else in his life: the simple enjoyment and, over and over, the possibility of winning. Start over. Start over. Start over. Every push of the button was a fresh chance. You could win at life, or at least know what that felt like.

Now he felt all of that, magnified by a thousand. But it was like everything had been turned inside out. He realized that this joy and possibility were not only part of the Casino but part of the entire world. The Casino *was* the world. It was thrilling. He felt as though the portal of the universe had opened up to him and he could see it all, its workings, its endlessness, its unknowability. But it was a glorious unknowability, an unknowability that he wanted to count on. Maybe, just maybe, the universe offered *something* rather than nothing. He wanted to live the rest of his life based on an assumption of somethingness, rather than nothingness, as he had always done before.

The trick was not to lose too much.

4.

In total, he stayed at the casino hotel for five days and four nights. Although he hadn't really thought it through, it was an ideal place to run away to. There were comfortable hotel rooms to sleep in and three restaurants, one of which featured the American diner food he loved. The waitresses—especially the kind angel, Maria—knew his name and remembered his order (in the morning: sausage, eggs, blueberry pancakes). Unlike his wife and daughter, they smiled at him and treated him kindly. And, of course, there were the slot machines, hundreds of them, spinning and flashing and beeping day and night, to keep him occupied for hours on end.

His wife and son had shown up late that first night, while he was drinking a Coke and up by almost two hundred dollars at a machine with particularly beautiful graphics. They said they had just guessed he would be there. But for some reason, there was a police officer standing several feet behind them. Before the police officer left, he told them there was nothing he could do in this situation: he, Teh-chang, was an adult, and no one was in danger or being harmed (he could have told them all of that himself). After that, he was impatient with his wife. She was so grim about everything, so negative. He spoke loudly. Maybe he was yelling. He just wanted her to be quiet. Why did she always want to control him? Why didn't she understand? At some point, he saw that his son was crying as he had not cried since he was a small child. He didn't really feel worried, though. It was okay for people to cry.

Finally they left, with an agreement that his son would come back the following day to bring him some requested items from home. He did not trust them, though, so he insisted on writing up a contract, which two of the front-desk clerks agreed to sign as witnesses. Under these circumstances, it was important to have things in writing.

Day 3, 6:10 a.m., handwritten contract on Pala Casino stationery, signed by Edward (Teh-chang) Cheng and desk clerks "Adriana" and "Tay":

"I did not have sleeping pajama, and felt cold in the room, and had to have higher temperature in the room in order to sleep—I never ask my wife to bring that to me. And when my son brought the thing I asked my wife to bring to me I got all things. Pajamas was not the thing I asked and I did not find it. That is okay."

On Day 3, he wrote on the family webpage: "I have escaped from my family to look for a single person who would believe me."

On Day 4, he emailed his family:

> Dear love and children, I am okay. Thanks my love for the understanding, and [my son] for coming to see me and talk to me. I have a lot of fun in the evening after

> taking a nap and dinner. I plan to stay one more night here as I have developed a theory for having fun playing the slot machines. I will need to write it down, and do some testing here. I will get a complimentary night for tonight. So come to have lunch with me tomorrow. Then we go home together. If you have time, perhaps I can show you how to enjoy playing the slot machines. It is really easy and fun.

5.

On Day 5, he went home. For the first time since his surgery, he felt a bit tired. That was okay. There was always tomorrow.

Gradually, over the weeks to come, he subsided back into his old self.

The sheen of the world, its brightness and clarity and endless possibility, dulled and shrank back down into daily routines, circumscribed geographies.

His house.

The orange trees in front of his house.

The road to town and back.

The road to the reservoir and back.

The road to the stop sign and back.

The road, a few gravel driveways down, to the fence post, where he had to stop and lean on his cane and wait for his daughter to walk back home to get the car and pick him up.

The driveway, with his walker, and with the help of Theresa, the assistant his wife hired after they decided he would stay at home and not go to the hospital anymore. He learned a new English word: *hospice*, as though it were a combination of "hospital" and "peace."

The room and the adjacent corridor to the bathroom.

The room.

The bed.

The bed.

The bed.

You can't turn around and escape the black hole.

But when you think about it, we all know that feeling, not from our experience with space but with time. Time only goes forwards, never backwards, and it pulls us along against our will, preventing us from turning around.

Toward the end, there was just so much silence. His wife and son and daughter and friends came and went. Theresa and his wife fed him, spoonful by spoonful. Theresa and his wife changed his adult diaper. Theresa and his wife gave him crushed-up morphine pills that turned his pureed food bitter. It was okay. He couldn't taste the food anyway. It was all texture now, unbearable texture to be forced down in order to live.

They eased him up to a sitting position with some difficulty and stuck fentanyl patches onto his bare back, underneath the threadbare white V-neck undershirt he wore all the time now. He tried to remember when his wife had first bought him that undershirt. It was probably twenty years ago now.

Twenty years ago his children were teenagers. Twenty years ago there was still so much ahead of all of them. He wanted to talk to his wife, but he didn't know what to say. Hadn't he thought about and said everything already? He had written it out in his poems over the past dozen or so years, over two hundred of them.

He thought of the last two stanzas of one of the forty poems his daughter had helped him to translate into English. The title of the poem was "Visiting Old Places to Say Goodbye to the Past."

> I returned to a place where a life began
> to say goodbye to the past,
> recalling an era,
> the last of a memory.
>
> Memories of a snow country
> (those are the most vivid)
> are deeply embedded in my heart
> (Let's bury them).
> Instead, bring the expectation of spring,
> with completely new hopes.
> Don't look back,
> while boarding a vessel of fate
> headed toward an unknown destination.

In those poems, he had written everything he could not say.

Wasn't that enough? He just wanted people to talk to him. Not ask him for things, not be disappointed with him, not talk about things that didn't really matter, just talk to him.

"Tell me a story," he asked his daughter.

"I can't think of any stories," she answered. She was tired, distracted. She looked toward the doorway.

His first grandchild was born to his son and daughter-in-law. Mako. He was named after a shark, a Maori word. But it was also the name of a Japanese princess, and all their Taiwanese friends were confused. The baby's Chinese name, chosen by his wife, made more sense: Pei-chi. "Pei" for abundant, "Chi" for strange, unexpected; for Chilai, one of the tallest mountains in Taiwan, where he and his wife had hiked when they were young and falling in love. The mountain where, a year after they met and he was doing his required military service, his wife had gone with their friends and nearly died in a typhoon. (Everyone else died except for her and one other person.) Had they cheated fate then?

He never said these things out loud, but he wondered.

What if his wife had died on Chilai, before they were married, before their son and daughter were born?

What if he had never regained consciousness on that rainy day sixty years ago when, running to school, he had slipped and hit his head?

What if he had quit smoking five years earlier, ten years earlier?

And so on.

His son put the baby at the foot of his bed. He was a round, fuzzy creature, all cheeks and drool. He looked like his son had, so many years ago. If only they could start over too.

"Mako," he called. "Mako." The tenderness in his own voice surprised him.

6.

The laws of physics require that you be both outside the black hole in a pile of ashes and inside the black hole alive and well.

There is no paradox, because no one person ever sees your clone. There's no observer who can see both inside and outside a black hole simultaneously. So, no laws of physics are broken.

Unless, that is, you demand to know which story is really true. Are you really dead or are you really alive?

On the last night, his daughter read to him. She read him the entire summary of *The Epic of Gilgamesh*, a story he had loved. She told him back the stories of Sun Wukong, that immortal trickster monkey, which he had told her and his son when they were children. She got a lot of the details wrong, but that was okay.

He couldn't see her anymore, could only hear her now and then.

His wife spoke to him in Taiwanese. Her voice was steady. "It's okay. You can go now." She held his hand.

He breathed. His breath was the universe.

In and out.

In.

And out.

In.

Out.

In-

The great secret is that there is no reality. Reality depends on whom you ask. End of story. Well, almost.

There will be many things to happen.
Just be quiet and wait and see.
I will be all right.

Originally published in The Cincinnati Review

Winner of The 2021 *Best Spiritual Literature* Award in Nonfiction
Selected by Molly McCully Brown

Broderick Eaton

Eulogy to a Tree

An unconscious alarm buried deep in my survival brain has pinged my senses just as I'm dropping from the barren burn scar down into the trees. I quickly scroll through my memory of the last few seconds, searching for some out of place sound or maybe the quick peripheral movement of a coyote dodging through the bitterbrush and burnt stumps. Something has made me pause halfway down from the ridge where I've been running with Atlas, the third big trail dog of my adult life. Dogs mean trail time and trail time means not just living but slowing the pace of everything else as feet or bike tires speed up, and seeing, breathing, smelling the dirt, hearing it crunch satisfyingly under knobbled traction during the push for an endorphin high that is always tantalizingly just ahead. I reached that high space twenty minutes ago where the trail is flat and fast, where pain subsides and thoughts unwind. Dirt and exertion bring clarity and calm. Down the rocky trail, Atlas stops to look back at me curiously. His large black shape is getting harder to see as night seeps across the air now that the sun has descended behind the mountains, leaving the sky singed magenta and shot through with gold.

Maybe it's the lack of sound that caught my attention; silence can be as loud as the commotion it replaces. Construction has begun on a new development west of our neighborhood on the edge of town, in the area that has been my daily refuge from the unrelenting pressures of work and kids and noise. Each empty lot is selling for no less than a million dollars, more if someone wants the windows of their future house to take in the generous view offered up here of the carpets of deep greens that imperceptibly turn to indigo and then purple as forests approach the piebald Cascades toothing the horizon. The view that has been all mine, so devastating in its untouched beauty that it has squeezed the labored breath from my body thousands of times in the last twenty years as I ran and biked these trails with Ruckus, then Daisy, and now Atlas.

For these twenty years, I have planned runs to end before the sun goes down so that we're back in civilization before the coyotes emerge from the sage to sing their reclamation of the land for the night. Lately, I wait until dusk to head out so we avoid encounters with rumbling yellow Caterpillars and Deere and men who spit tobacco-stained comments about the size of my dog and being out there alone—reminding me why I run with a dog who could easily be mistaken for Cerberus in the first place. When Atlas and I started out this evening, there were still machines snarling down a newly torn stretch, growing ever closer as they chopped every tree within reach to clear the area for building. A road will soon lead expensive cars to their expensive driveways. So we headed into the trees in the opposite direction and now a late silence settles after the day's dust as we descend into the space where they were working. The drum of my heart hammering a gradually slowing rhythm, I place my hand on the trunk of the closest ponderosa to keep my balance as I stretch. Beneath my fingers the jigsaw bark is rough, yet its contours invite my fingers to each individually find a groove to rest in. The cessation of noise makes the quiet that much more complete and, for a moment, my breath is the only sound louder than my pulse.

I look up into the pine branches that fan sparsely around the trunk. Sprays of long spines needle the sky's purpling finale. It's not a particularly thick tree, but it must be significantly older than I am. The growing climate in the eastern foothills of the Cascades is stingy at best; winter starts in October and can last into June. Some years, the cold is gentle, and the following spring brings acres of tiny fuchsia and yellow flowers to cover the desert east of town. Other years, temperatures can stay below zero for days if not weeks, solidifying the soil well beyond the reach of roots and causing cleared snow piled at the sides of neighborhood driveways in great amorphous lumps that only begin to dwindle once the daffodils have sprung up in May.

But the greatest accomplishment of this tree is that it is alive at all. A few years ago, a wildfire broke out a couple of miles from our house. Technically, fire season hadn't even started yet, but two columns of smoke roiled into the pristine

June sky and cast an eerie shadow over the street where my boys were riding their bikes. Overnight, the fire gorged on already dry fuels and grew from two hundred acres to six thousand and we packed the cars and prepared the kids for what evacuation might look like. But through constant retardant drops by a newly commissioned jet that droned overhead all night and the grace of the wind the next day, the danger was contained before it reached civilization or this patch of trees that stands as an oasis in a wide bare swath created by a similar moment in my youth.

From the evidence gathered in the aftermath thirty years ago that led to the arrest and prosecution of a firebug disguised as a hero, details emerged that take little imagination to put to story:

Already an arsonist deep in his burning heart, the wildland firefighter stands up from the log he's using as a chair in the campsite he calls home. The season is coming to an end and while local residents breathe a sigh of relief that this wasn't the year our worst fears came to life, his firefighting business is failing as a result of our good fortune. Ponderosa and juniper forest around him thickly softens both sides of the shallow valley cut by Tumalo Creek. So wild, so tantalizingly close to developed areas, so necessary to hire firefighters to keep a spark from burning into town. Undergrowth of bitterbrush and manzanita grows heavily and has dried out over the hot summer with little rain. It's so parched that it almost crackles just looking at it. A small dust devil kicks up from Shevlin Park down below and twists away into the blue. Heat and wind...perfect. He looks at the cigarette nearing its end at his fingertips. With a flick, it lands and begins to sizzle in a patch of wheat-colored foxtails. He gets ready for the call.

It's August of 1990. The Awbrey Hall fire churns at the west edge of town with the terrifying speed and sound of a locomotive. It starts around 3:00 on an early August Saturday afternoon, and by 3:00 the next morning it has traveled six miles to the south, devouring twenty-two homes and incinerating thousands of acres. It burns so fast in patches that some trees are left partially alive, and so hot in others that nothing but smoldering ash is left and trees and home sidings are burned just from close proximity to the inferno. Weather conditions feed the fire when a hot wind picks up and the temperature doesn't drop at night the way it usually does at this altitude. City and wildland firefighters unite, using main roads and a highway as firebreaks that should give them a chance to slow the fire's progress. Instead, the blaze effortlessly leaps across their silly human attempts, sending magnificent comets across the night sky. Where embers land, new flames burst to life and the fire races on, tracing a straight north-south line more than the length of city limits. All the firefighters keep at the edge of their thoughts the impossible disaster of what would happen if the voracious wind changed and the six-mile wall of fire shifted toward town. This is before cell phones and reverse 911, so several of my friends and their families have just enough time to evacuate after a frantic knock on the door by the sheriff telling them to leave everything and go. Every person who experiences this gives the same description of the unbelievable sound: the roar of a freight train bearing down on their homes. I miss all the drama because I am living in Costa Rica on a summer exchange program, but in a handful of phone calls home I learn that my family temporarily houses a young couple displaced by the fire that burns along the entire length of the western edge of town with such ferocity that little is left in its wake. It finally stops when the wind shifts and turns the fire back onto the area it has already burned, giving personnel a chance to gain the upper hand and leaving the flames to die out with no fuel.

For the people and wildlife in the path of the fire, Fate sweeps through and points her wand; the luck of some people means their homes and lives stay intact, while the luck of others means disaster strikes in an instant and they lose everything.

This tree under my hand is a miracle. It was spared the random bad luck that struck down an entire forest that used to blanket the ridge I've just run down on my way back to a neighborhood built well after the Awbrey Hall fire. Along with about fifty other trees in this protected pocket, this ponderosa repopulated the area, though the "new" trees are still—at thirty years old—only about six feet tall with trunks no bigger around than my thigh and there is still far more empty space than forest.

I consider the luck of this tree and its important role as parent to a new generation, and how this luck has run its course as the encroachment of development has now determined an unnatural end for all of these trees that survived what should have been the worst threat. Fate has a funny way of surprising us when we least expect it, of upending the status quo and sending us tumbling into a different reality. It turns us into trees rooted helplessly in place as wildfire roars toward us.

The first time my father announces he has cancer I hold my tiny son—the first grandson—against my heart to keep it from exiting my chest forever. I can't feel my hands for three days. My most useful appendages, cut off by this news. Suddenly, the focus placed on the myriad details of life changes to a fight for the survival of what we know. These details become meaningless under the sickly yellow light of a smoke cloud that has just passed in front of our sun. Within a few weeks, though, resulting prostate surgery and scans turn out to be far less traumatic than we were braced for and we pedal on down the trail, oblivious to the fact that we have stomped out only the first ember blown at us from a firestorm building out of sight.

The second time my father announces he has cancer the shock is less. We've done this before. This time, it's in his esophagus, probably the product of smoking since his teen years. Now I have a second grandson for him and the two of them are age-disparate clones who adore each other. Through infusions and drug cocktails we begin to learn the chemical language of treatment. Radiation targets his throat while chemotherapy poisons his blood and steroids prop up the parts that flag in immune system exhaustion. When the numbers that mean success or failure aren't changing as expected, surgeons remove his larynx and a handful of lymph nodes from his neck. Grandsons play with the microphone held to his throat that becomes Grandpa's voice in their small memories while the rest of us dance around the word "cancer"—a word you can physically feel burrowing into your very marrow, attacking like a virus every cell, every thought, every second that limps by wondering *what if…?* It is a word that effortlessly shatters the sense of immortality we all suffer from until we are brought face to face with the specter of our end.

Summer arrives in all its baking glory and we go to Yellowstone and Grand Teton as we do every three years, visiting our favorite locations on Jackson Lake, in the geyser basins, and along the Firehole River. We were there during the massive fires in 1988, watching as flames evaporated all the landmarks we recognized. When we left that year, the hills surrounding the Old Faithful basin glowed orange at night. We were back home by the time the fires converged and descended on Old Faithful Inn. News footage showed firefighters, barely visible through the thick smoke, crouched on the shake roof of the big log structure, spraying it with foam until white streams dripped from its eaves. As night fell and flames narrowed the small circle of buildings and trucks visible only by their flashing lights, it looked like the building was lost. My mother turned off the television and we went to bed in tears, sure the old lodge would be burned to the ground by morning.

But miracles happen. Mom woke us up early to tell us that firefighters had stayed at Old Faithful, risking their lives as the firestorm blew into the basin, to battle the blaze through the night. While most of the trees and some outbuildings were gone, our beloved Inn was still standing. Like those of our hometown, the trees in Yellowstone are slow to grow in the high altitude and long winters. Each trip since then, we note changes, delight in new green that covers the burned land on the next trip, and revel in the recovery of what we thought was lost.

On this trip, with Dad in treatment, burns of his own encircle his neck and spread down his shoulders. Radiation has taken a serious turn, making him cold in the painful summer sun, and the steroids leave him unusually out of sorts. I am equally out of sorts, months into my pregnancy with the family's third grandson and miserable in the summer heat. We are both uncomfortable and argue over the use of heat or air conditioning in the car. He wins, of course, because how could he not? We are facing diametrically opposing ends of the life arc in our conditions.

Many months later, a new word, one made of cooling waters, enters our vocabulary and douses our fears: remission. Dad has survived the fire, we've all made it through, and we can look forward to recovery from this rough patch.

The third time my father announces he has cancer we have barely had time—less than a year—to find our footing. A lymph node, brightly lit by boron that glows during a scan, had escaped the oncologist's notice and has been quietly spreading disease through previously healthy tissue. A new scan shows several lymph nodes involved now, plus an inoperable spot on his lung. Like wildfire, cancer is opportunistic and will spread in whichever direction it finds the fuel to take hold. It will devour whatever is unlucky enough to be caught in its path.

The shells of my parents pack up this diagnosis into exhausted brains and hearts that aren't yet able to fully absorb such words and they leave the doctor's office to enter a world blithely operating as usual around them. Cars still drive past. Dogs still bark. They still need milk in the refrigerator. The afternoon sun still rests on their backs and casts shadows onto the concrete of the two of them standing next to each other. On their way home they stop at BiMart for their usual errands, going through the paces as though their foundation and future have not just crumbled into dust around them. They carry this terminal news into the store to buy whatever temporary items seem so necessary in that moment. They have yet to realize how precious every movement is. At the checkout, Dad notices that his member number has been drawn as a winner that day. His prize is a bag of pretzels.

"Hey, it's my lucky day!" he exclaims as the cashier hands over the snacks that no one will ever eat, and the dark irony of the situation settles over them. There is nothing in the cashier's manual that addresses protocol on how to handle two people who burst into inconsolable tears after winning a bag of pretzels.

We carry on living because our hearts keep marching and our blood drives our feet forward. My husband listens and holds me when my grief runs over because he has never seen a wildfire burning up someone's recognizable life and he doesn't know what else to do. There is no manual for guidance on grasping at a lifelong foundation that suddenly has turned to quicksilver while at the same time celebrating the arrival of new life and trying to pull the two into the same embrace. Grabbing sleep whenever I can with an infant, my rest is overheated and full of intense dreams that are the result of an overworked mind trying to process the impossible information forcing its way in. One sticks uncomfortably to me for days:

I'm standing on a dark stage, next to a man in the center of a spotlight. I can't see his face because he's backlit in light that is soft and welcoming yet with an intensity that is blinding. Around him on the floor are scattered cue cards with words on them. The words are printed in large, black typeface and he's searching anxiously for something. I stoop and begin to pick up the words, stacking them in my arms because I know this is what he's looking for. I finish collecting the words and wave to get the man's attention. As he turns, a happiness that feels a lot like love flows to me in an overwhelming force that has always connected us, and I recognize him. I hand him the words one by one and notice that most of them are things he has pronounced wrong for as long as I can remember. I hold my arms wider for the last word that is printed in larger font than the others. He reverberates with appreciation and hugs the cards close to his chest as I look down and see the last word: speaking.

His words are gone with his larynx, but I know what he wants to say. I know this by every action he makes with what is left of his body. The measurements he takes for bunk beds as his head grows big from fluids trapped by the removal of lymph nodes in his neck, and his athletic legs grow unfamiliarly skinny from the poisons meant to kill the cancer but taking the rest of his tissues in the process, both of us aware that the chances of his completing the project are slim. His grandsons snuggle in for whispered stories and don't know any different. Like anyone who gets to know the area west of town after the fire, this is just how their forest looks and sounds.

The next summer, we move the national parks trip up by a year. Dad insists on going to all the hikes and viewpoints with us, though he is quick to volunteer to stay at trailheads with my youngest boys and my sister with her baby son. The head of Old Faithful Inn's porters, an angel named Gabriel with a deep understanding of the burning up of valuable treasures, takes my parents on a special tour up through the interior log rafters and out onto the Inn's roof for the evening retrieval and folding of the American flag. He stands back as the two of them pause at the railing to look out over the geyser basin that has been our family's playground for so many years, where steam hovers like spirits and the forest has slowly regrown to crowd the surrounding hills in low green that hides the devastation from twenty-one years before. Back downstairs, we gather in the evenings for cocktails and spend hours talking on the balcony, measuring time only by periodic eruptions of the proverbial geyser. These moments are predictable and allow us to feel normal for a short respite.

I don't know what possesses me, but when we have the cars in the front portico to pack up on the last morning, I am moved to take a picture of my dad's brown Yukon, surrounded by the life-sized Lincoln Log structure of our favorite building, as Old Faithful erupts in the background. It's as if our family's "summer home" is saying goodbye with a flourish and I must capture the moment in a photo.

Two weeks after we arrive back home, he is hospitalized with a sudden, high fever. With all his antibodies stolen away by chemo, his blood has gone septic and we don't know for a few hours if he will survive. His diminished body barely takes up space in the hospital bed.

Like a shift in the wind when fire is racing ahead, new drugs stop the infection, pull him from the precipice, and prop him back on his feet. He and my mom and my siblings continue preparations to leave for Europe so Dad can check Normandy off the top of his bucket list after visiting Rome and the hills of Tuscany. I will stay home to get the year launched at the school I run. The day before they leave, his doctor signs off on his numbers—he's healthy enough to fly. My parents come to my house to say goodbye, though it's really an excuse to hug their grandsons. Thin and pale as he stands on the sun-warmed wood of my kitchen floor, he sways slightly like a January aspen with its lifesap drawn so far into its core that its naked branches have taken on a dry, papery gray. The aspen that won't come back from this last winter.

In a flash of sacred knowledge that doesn't require words, I know this is the last time we will say goodbye to each other. I think I should be honored to recognize this moment, but it sends my heart into arrhythmic panic. I don't say anything because it would dampen everyone's excitement, and maybe, just maybe, I'm wrong. Everyone chatters around us and all I can do is stare at the fragile shell that vaguely resembles my father as my insides melt with helplessness. I see him deep inside himself, searching through the garden of his tissues for the last weeds that keep him rooted to this earth. He's pulling them out.

They make their way to the door, the porch, the car. My mother reads my face and scurries past, chirping brightly again that she wishes we could be going with them. I pick up my youngest son and hold him against my heart as the car backs out and drives off so that I won't run after them and ask for another goodbye. I watch my mother intentionally looking ahead, avoiding my face because she has seen what I saw. They round the corner and I stand there with the soft body of my son in my arms, his sweet breath on my neck as he reaches a pudgy finger up to trace a tear down my cheek. In a world that is somehow still spinning, afternoon sun creeps across the porch and warms the wood planks beneath my feet.

On a bluebird September morning a few days later, I call my friend Patrik for a gravity ride. Patrik grew up with my sister and knows my parents and my husband; he is family. He understands my need to be in the mountains where the shush of dirt under bike tires soothes my wilding mind, where my heart has a reason to pound so hard, where trees stay in place and I can fly among them. Normally we ride with my sister and brother-in-law, but they are in Italy where Dad quietly left his body in a hospital in Arezzo. Sepsis. The business of transporting remains from the other side of the world is slow and they will not return for almost a week. Patrik and I don't talk much in the truck on the way to where the trail starts, next to eternally frigid bodies of water right in the glaciered cradle between two mountains miles above town. We clip our helmets and tighten our packs, then turn our wheels east from the spot where nine months later, after the snowpack has pulled back its cold fingers, the remains of my family will quietly return to sow the earth with ashes. From the lakes we climb slowly to warm up, letting our muscles spin out of their sleep and prepare themselves to grind. The trail is damp after a quick late summer thunderstorm and our cadence picks up in anticipation. I turn my heart rate monitor off because I do not want to know what my heart has to say. We crest the ridge next to Tumalo Mountain and the descent begins. Faster and faster our wheels turn until we are bright lycra blurs flashing through the shadows of old growth fir and spruce. This is hero dirt at its finest, real holy rolling on clingy dark loam that begs us to let it all go. Can I open it up to 25 miles per hour? How fast is too fast to live? Would it matter if I kept pedaling and rocketed off the planet into the place that burnt up trees and loved ones drift to when they're gone?

I quiet these thoughts; my roots are still spread wide and deep. I will stay here and live the sweet devastation of a thin trail, a meaningless line in the Cascades that is the only thing that matters to me right now. Then I will return to the boys who wait for me to come back through the door. I will do this for them today, because one day, I won't. I swoop an unbanked turn at 26 miles per hour. I have to keep spinning or nothing will make any sense. Pressing the chain to its last gear, I ask my searing legs for more. It is spiritual, hurtling back toward town, toward a reality I do not want to face. Gravity is the only truth here. As I hit 32 miles per hour the trail drops into the watershed where it clings to Tumalo Creek as though looking for guidance down the mountain. I don't know how long the wasp has been inside my jersey, but it is there next to the tumbling water, just before we enter the bare expanse left by the Awbrey Hall fire nineteen years before, that I feel a sting on my stomach, and then another before the burning kicks in. I shout to Patrik, slide my bike to the ground and race to get Benadryl from my pack to stop the coming allergic reaction. As huge, angry welts bloom across my abdomen, I embrace the only real thing I will feel for weeks.

Pulse slowing, the chuffing steam engine in my chest has returned to normal as the pine tree and I hold each other up. Darkness deepens even as I watch. I press my fingers into the bark and revel in the growing sense of sharpness digging into the flesh of my fingers. Down the trail, in the trees beyond Atlas, a great-horned owl softly starts its hollow-throated call. I stop breathing to hear it better, and a woody reply sounds behind me, higher up toward the ridge where purple is giving way to near-black as night pushes in from the continent's Great Basin to our east. The large yellow grader, finished for the day, ticks in the shadows out of sight as its engine cools. Geese clamor in the distance. Atlas alerts and I follow his gaze to where the horizon above us undulates with the barely-there silhouettes of a handful of deer startled into fleeing. They are visible because the trees in that space burned away all those years ago. I place my other hand on the trunk and press it between my palms in the same way I do to my children's faces. I imagine I can feel its cellulose pulse as it draws from the earth and gives to the sky. *I'm sorry, friend. You survived the fire, but you won't survive us. Let us both perform this act of living while we can.* I release the tree, whistle to Atlas, and we turn toward home.

Winner of The 2021 *Best Spiritual Literature* Award in Poetry
Selected by Leila Chatti

B. Tyler Lee

And All God's Queer Girls Said Amen

as they hummed the Doxology like they were
stuffing biscuits in their pockets. Then they ate
lamb's body, dry against their teeth as an old
rugged cross, and washed it down with Concord
blood. The queer girls swallowed a lot of things:
iced tea and sugar beans, tales of the single pastor's
chastity, belts across their thighs, diet pills, daddy
longlegs on dares, the pastors' breath in the darkened
fellowship hall, honeysuckle nectar, theories
about their hymens and chewing gum.
They
sang "Be Thou My Vision" and the praises
of the oak paddles their fathers carved by hand,
the custom grooves for their mothers' fingers.
And on Wednesday nights, when the women's
choir leader gathered her babies from the church
nursery and shook down her bun like honey
in July, they whispered it again: "Praise God
from whom all blessings flow."
At home
they would slice the burnt crust from the skillet
cornbread for their little sisters and brothers,
wishing only for warm molasses and whole milk,
ignoring the iron weight of Leviticus around

their waists. *So be it,* they thought—of Texas
sheet cakes and control top tights, of the choir
leader's robust soprano and one another. *So be it.*

Kenji C. Liu

A Specter Is Haunting Street View

1.

I am stalking our old house on Google Street View. Lawn, driveway, car. I am not sure if this view is from before, during, or after. You might still linger there behind the windows. If I could see in. These past months, you have vanished and vanished, and now I cannot follow.

Zoom out into the clouds overhead, an airplane in midair, fragmented and whole. Mom, you cannot be made to exist.

2.

In Japanese, verbs can take passive and causative passive forms. Instead of “I see you,” there is mirareru, which translates as “seeing happens” (“見られる), or misaserareru, “seeing can be made to happen” (“見させられる). Instead of “I don’t see you,” there is mirarenai, which translates as “seeing does not happen” (“見られない), or misaserarenai, “seeing cannot be made to happen” (“見させられない). The act of seeing (or not) occurs, due to a reason that may (or may not) be discernible.

3.

I propose that every map is haunted by a congress of ghosts, specters. Some are residents, installed there by the force of history. Others are wanderers, but drawn to a place by some crucial scent.

Since mapmakers decide what information to reveal, and especially what to hide, a map deals in specters. They are created through the application of power—hiding, closing, forgetting. An unseeing.

4.

Under the map is another map, a different way of understanding and navigating. Spectral maps with other place names, hierarchies of importance, ways of demarcating space, of prioritizing resources. A seeing that cannot be made to happen except through collective memory or initiation.

In the enclosure of the internet, too, there are different kinds of specters, the specters of satellite eyes and roaming cameras—the partial, not-fully-captured people in Google Street View. Twisted wisps, awkward fragments, people who are indescribable in three dimensions and so appear to fold, unfold, implode. People who have been written into a map, but in the edges, where monsters live. (De-augmented.)

5.

Using Google Street View, haunting can be made to happen. I haunt the places I have lived, because I want to catch a glimpse of them with and without me. I see traces that would eventually lead back to me—my car, the car of a loved one, a loved one taking out the trash. I exist in the network created by those objects and people, but not directly. I am implied because I was there. You are implied too. Now more than ever, you exist because of the spaces you used to exist in.

6.

Dear Mom—

With you, seeing does not happen. Seeing cannot be made to happen.

7.

Dad found our umbilical cord. Not my cord, but ours. A small, plain wood box containing white paper wrapped around almost-dust.

My birth hospital is located in Kyoto's northeast. Riding my computer mouse, I travel around the hospital's perimeter, follow a street to the delivery entrance, and peer up at a window. Zoom in. No presence in the window, but in the street there is a delivery man and the fragment of a walking woman, no shoulders and face. Google never leaves the face intact, a privacy consideration with ghostly effect.

My parents met as part of a church group in this part of Kyoto, so I hunt down nearby churches. I don't know which one it is, so I mark them all. The present version of the tenuous, possible past.

You are always implied wherever I am. Which end of the cord is still attached to you?

8.

The database Historic Aerials compiles historic aerial photographs and layers them with topographic maps, in the same way that Google Maps compiles satellite imagery. My childhood neighborhood's topography is viewable from 1888 to 1998, and aerial photographs are available from 1931 to the present. The New Jersey geography I grew up in but never really experienced—forests and swamps and farmland—I watch it get enclosed, bulldozed, built on. It is a flip book of colonization, suburban development, available in ghostly sequence.

Like the rest of North America, in New Jersey, everything is overlaid on top of Indigenous places. There are many Lenape names on the map—Metuchen, Hoboken, Piscataway, Secaucus—and major streets and highways often follow their original trails. Genocide haunts, it exists everywhere. Even if oblivious, we are made by these maps.

9.

At the edge of the map, where I met the Pacific Ocean to grieve, you once visited me in the shape of a harbor seal. A moment of rest in your dark, canine eyes. Is this not a kind of seeing, made to happen by the collusion of memory, longing, and some warm, self-organizing force?

10.

Before Pokémon Go and its predecessor game Ingress, there is the augmented-reality, location-based game Shadow Cities. Augmented reality is a thin digital reality mapped onto reality, a seeing that is made to happen. Teams compete to capture and hold territory by setting up beacons at portals, and teleport to other friendly beacons. A player might be sitting in a café, casually nurturing a local portal, and someone walking by on the street attacks it. Many games are colonization replayed.

Around October 2011, while I was engrossed in Shadow Cities, word spread that players were setting up beacons at 1 Infinite Loop Drive in Cupertino, California, Apple headquarters. I teleported in and landed among tens of dozens of bright towers of light springing up everywhere. A quick internet search revealed that Steve Jobs had died. A digital memorial haunting the digital location of a physical place, home to a corporation (which is itself a fiction) whose founder had passed away.

11.

Dear Mom—

You always had a lot of trouble staying awake in front of screens anyway.

12.

In 2014, Michael Brown is shot and killed by a white police officer in Ferguson, leading to weeks of unrest and revolt. In 2018, spurred by seemingly endless police murders of Black people—among them Lajuana Phillips, April Webster, DeAndre Ballard, Emantic Bradford, Jr., Stephon Clark, Andre Horton, Botham Jean, Jemel Roberson, and Antwon Rose—I visit the site of Brown's killing on Street View, curious if Google has recorded any trace of the protests. I go with some apprehension, wary of my own voyeurism, but I have been wondering how traces of violence might haunt the digital realm. A residential area. I angle the view upward to the sky and downward to the asphalt. Shadow Cities has shut down by this time, so I do not know if there are any digital memorials there, in the augmented world.

In Google Street View, captured July 2016, the street is empty but rip mike brown is spray-painted along the curb three times, along with remnants of the word fuck. The June

2018 Street View of the site shows a pile of offerings on the street marking the spot, and another at the foot of a nearby streetlight. As of April 2021, remnants of rip, brown, and fuck are still visible.

In his testimony, the cop describes Brown as a "demon." He was shooting at a fiction in his own mind, making an unarmed, eighteen-year-old Black man who had just graduated from high school into a superhuman specter. Claudia Rankine: "Because white men can't / police their imagination / black men are dying."

Ferguson is founded by settler-colonists in 1855. The region now known as the state of Missouri is the traditional lands of the Illinois Confederation, a nation decimated by war, European disease, and conquest. Until the 1960s, the city strives to keep Black people out via policing, redlining, and physical barriers. Before Brown's neighborhood is built between 1969 and 1971, it is a golf course. By the time of Brown's murder, the neighborhood is majority Black. To overlay these different maps—to purposefully augment your own reality with history, memory—is to become haunted. To do this and not be destroyed, to let the tension move you and bring you closer to others, this is a kind of seeing that can be made to happen.

13.

Looking is not the same as seeing. Many things pass through

the sense door of sight. Most we ignore. Many we have our own stories about, regardless of reality. In very rare cases, we see them as they actually are, without footnotes. We see them as they truly are, and perhaps they change us.

14.

I would like to be made aware of everything that has happened in a place. I would like seeing to happen, to be made to happen. That is the price of living in a place like the United States, which has such a short historical memory, and expends amazing amounts of energy to make it even shorter. It might seem like a way to escape, to shorten your shadow until you are a single eye on a stick. To shrink into the center of a cage in an attempt to escape it. Life trying to escape itself.

15.

Haunted by what you ignore and unable to understand why, you wander.

Originally published in Ecotone

Winner of The 2021 *Best Spiritual Literature* Award in Fiction Selected by SJ Sindu

Nancy Ludmerer

The Loneliness Cure

Some people never feel lonely. Their own thoughts shield them from loneliness and wretchedness. What thoughts? That is a secret known only to the non-lonely. Each has a different secret, a different thought. It's enough to know that these people can be anywhere—an empty house, a prison cell, a road so dark and deserted it gleams, a graveyard—and still not feel bereft.

Others are lonely all the time, even when surrounded by voices, by the clatter of knives and forks, by noisy chewing, by chickens squawking under the knife, by praying and singing, by chattering seamstresses, by babies crying, and, in a town like ours, by meddlers who know everyone's business. Meddlers who think the only cure for loneliness is marriage, without realizing that marriage creates a loneliness all its own.

The last time I heard Hannah Rochel preach, she said being alone was nothing to fear. Jacob was alone when he wrestled with the angel. "And what happened after?" she asked the empty anteroom, which only weeks before had been filled with nearly a hundred women, thirty-odd men. Now I was her only follower. I waited in silence, though I knew the answer. "The angel blessed him." Soon perhaps there would be no one to hear her. I was 22 and finally getting married. My wedding was a week away. I didn't know what that would mean for my relationship with Hannah Rochel Verbermacher.

Seven years earlier, when she purchased the three-story building for her Beit Midrash, Hannah Rochel showed me the deed, her eyes shining: the boundaries of the property in pale ink; a simple hand-drawn sketch showing the square brick structure on Sokalska street; her signature and the seller's signature in darkest blue; the date bearing an ornate 1822, the "2"s curled like snakes. A multitude of official seals: the humble black seal of our town, Volodymyr-Volynsky; the red seal of the province of Volhynia; the gold seal of Imperial Russia; and the stern profile of Tsar Alexander, annointed in 1806, the year of Hannah Rochel's birth. His Excellency tightened Mother Russia's grip on the Jews of Poland, but neither Hannah Rochel nor I—mere babies at the time—knew anything about that.

Although my mother told me about Hannah Rochel Verbermacher when I was growing up, I didn't actually meet her until I was 14 and my brother Chaim, whom I looked after, was almost 7. I had gone to pick up Chaim from Cheder, where he studied Torah with boys who ranged from 5 to 13. Hannah Rochel looked about my age (it turned out she was only 12) but was smaller, lean and boyish, with silky translucent skin, chestnut colored hair that fell in curls, and wide-apart blue-grey eyes. I was large and ungainly, red-haired and freckled. I dragged my right foot; my right eye was called lazy though it worked twice as hard to keep up with the left; and my skin, in spite of or because of the freckles, was mottled and grey-looking. Hannah Rochel looked at me, really looked, and then looked at Chaim, her unlikely classmate given the age and gender difference (and she the most unlikely of Cheder students, allowed to pursue her studies there only as a courtesy to her father.) She said, "I knew you had to be Chaim's sister. He is smart and sweet, and you, Tirzah, are the same." I wondered how she knew my name.

Hannah Rochel had no brothers (or sisters either, for that matter), whereas I had an older brother, Nachshon, and two younger ones. I rarely saw Nachshon any more. During the week, he studied at a Yeshivah in Lublin, where he stayed with a local family, and only occasionally came home for Shabbos dinner and the weekend. In addition to Chaim, there was a two-year-old boy—David. I cleaned up their messes, mended their clothes, even cooked their meals. My mother worked as a midwife and was on call day and night. She was known for her skill with first-time mothers, especially inexperienced girls who had no younger siblings to tend to. She knew how to soothe sick or colicky infants; help girls when their monthly bleeding was painful or clotted; help their mothers during *the changes*, which—unlike babies—occurred, she said, when no one expected them.

My father studied most of the time. When he wasn't studying, he tutored boys who were slow or difficult, which made it all the more important that his own sons be scholars. My parents praised me but privately I believe they despaired. They knew that the less desirable girls in our town were destined to be married off, eventually, to the widowers, the old, the infirm. Why didn't my mother train me for her profession? I never asked because I knew the answer. I was born with two disabilities—eye and limb; what woman giving birth would want to be tended by me? Sometimes I wondered why God caused me to suffer not one, but two impairments. But then I thought, who am I to think God considers me for even one second? Of course, He does not.

The day I met Hannah Rochel I did something I had never done. Before Chaim and I began our walk home, while Hannah Rochel stood smiling at us, I asked Chaim what he had learned in Cheder that day and he said, hopping from foot to foot, "we learned about Gerizim and Ebal." I asked him to explain as if I wished to know and while part of me did, I also wished to remain basking in Hannah Rochel's attention. She continued to appraise me. What did she see? I couldn't think of that.

Chaim explained that Gerizim and Ebal were two peaks in the same mountain range, composed of the same soil and rock and watered by the same rain and dew. Yet Ebal was barren and Gerizim covered with fruit trees. One was curses and one was blessings. I said, carelessly, "Sounds like your teacher gave you a good and meaningful lesson."

He looked stunned, "Not our teacher. *Hannah Rochel.* She's the one who teaches us. Moreh tries, but by the afternoon he is too tired. Sometimes he falls asleep standing up, like a horse!" He laughed and Hannah Rochel smiled. I could say nothing.

My mother attended Hannah Rochel's birth. Many town residents couldn't afford a midwife (or thought they couldn't, not knowing my mother would, if needed, work for free). Hannah Rochel's parents were rich. Monesh Verbermacher began life as a weaver, but became a merchant of fine cloth and other commodities; one of the most successful men in Volodymyr-Volynsky—except in the most important way. After ten years, Monesh and his wife Mirla were childless. A rabbi urged Monesh to seek a divorce but he wouldn't. He loved Mirla; besides, that would be to admit his failure. For the same reason, he refused to go on a pointless trek to consult the seer of Chernobyl, a so-called miracle worker. Monesh thought it nonsense that the rebbe could achieve what his nights and Shabbat afternoons with Mirla could not.

Monesh knew the prayers but he was not religious.

Mirla was desperate. She went on the journey, as she warned Monesh she would, with only a maidservant for company. They traveled for miles. Mirla rode a fat compliant mare with a broad saddle; the maidservant walked alongside.

Sometimes they switched places. Of course, I heard this tale second-hand—or perhaps third- or fourth-hand. It's something Mirla Verbermacher told my mother, or told another midwife, who told my mother, or perhaps it was simply town gossip. I like to think Mirla spoke directly to my mother about her perilous journey during Hannah Rochel's birth. This is what I remember from my mother's telling: how the night grew chill, how they eventually saw the lights of the town where the rebbe lived. How his house was the grandest in the town but, as they approached, fog descended and shrouded it in darkness.

When it came time for them to appear before the rebbe, they trembled, first with fear, then with awe. They forgot the discomforts of the journey. The rebbe radiated a warm glow; adorned in velvet robes of indigo, he sat on a pillow on a golden chair. Mirla and the maidservant remained on the threshold; yet the light of his glow so dazzled them, they had to shield their eyes. The rebbe said Mirla should return home in joy; within the year she would have a baby! A brilliant child, who should be taught Torah and Prophets and Talmud, who should be brought up as a pious Jew, and who should be permitted to choose a mate, with no parental interference. What else the rebbe may have told Mirla is lost. Did he say it would be a girl? Not as the story came down to us.

My mother agreed with Monesh. She said that the idea that the rebbe had any influence was speculation or worse: chicanery. She said what you couldn't see, didn't exist. "What about love?" I recently asked her. She looked at me startled, and even a little afraid. Afraid perhaps because she feared she had underestimated me, had married me off to an older man, unhandsome, unromantic, even unrich. A master of "uns" yet still expressing kindness in his gaze, the curve of his cheek, his slightly bashful approach. But my marriage and that worried look from my mother—all that was nearly a decade in the future at the time I met Hannah Rochel. Hannah Rochel and I began to walk together each afternoon when I picked up Chaim from Cheder. This was lovely for me and even, I think, for Hannah Rochel. Her brilliance and odd ways were known around town; she debated the local rebbes (those brave enough to counter her) on Talmudic questions and more often than not prevailed; in the afternoons, while the boys' teacher slept the sleep of the righteous, she taught in his stead; at 12 she studied not only Torah and Prophets and Aggadot but the Zohar. She taught herself Hebrew and Aramaic and read all the sacred books in the original; the rest of us girls and women read them in Yiddish and then only the condensed editions with their morals and messages.

Hannah Rochel sat in the women's section during services but, starting a few months before I met her, donned a tallit—a fringed prayer shawl—and tefillin. Tefillin! A leather strap wrapped tight around her right forearm held in place a box with a small scroll in it; a leather strap around her high forehead did the same. These rites were learned by boys her age; when my brother Nachshon was learning to *lay tefillin* (for that is the expression) how odd he looked to me. I asked my father why the straps were bound so tight. He said, "to remember to follow God's commandments." Girls had no obligation to wear a tallit or lay tefillin; I guess someone thought our memories were better. But Hannah Rochel didn't care what girls were or were not required to do. She prayed at home that way, too. No one cared what she did at home. Indeed, they didn't care what she did in the women's section, either, so long as no one talked about it.

My father talked about it. He was one of those who disapproved. Her brilliance could not be disputed; it at least was God-given. But a girl, he said, especially one on the verge of womanhood, must not take on the obligations of a male—especially the wearing of tefillin. He put on tefillin every morning and prayed sequestered in a corner of the same room where he and my mother slept. Sometimes I was close by, attending to some chore, and observed him. After he heard about Hannah Rochel's practice, it seemed he wrapped the leather straps even tighter than before, working with a kind of fury, his eyes closed, his cheeks redder than usual. Was he willing away the image of Hannah Rochel doing the same?

Then one day Chaim asked if he could lay tefillin too.

"Not until you're twelve," my father said.

Chaim brightened. "Like Hannah Rochel!"

"No! Not like Hannah Rochel! Like me, like Nachshon. Hannah Rochel doesn't know what she's doing."

I wanted to defend my friend. But I didn't have the words or knowledge to do so.

My father saw that Hannah Rochel and I walked together. He asked what we spoke about. "Nothing important," I said. Hannah Rochel continued the discussion of Ebal and Gerizim; how it is up to us to choose—blessings or curses. We walked through the central square, past our 13th century Russian Orthodox cathedral; past the wooden synagogue and the Catholic church; past the infirmary, the square where the open-air market was held, past the prison. She slowed her pace to mine; my leg trailed behind us like a stray dog. A bearded man came towards us, another Jew, murmuring a blessing I had heard now and then from passersby since I was small: Baruch Atah Adonai, Eloheinu melech ha'olam, m'shaneh habriyot. *Blessed are You, Adonai our God, ruler of the universe, who makes creatures different.* I was that different creature. It was not meant to be cruel; but still made me feel marked.

"What did you say?" she asked the man, standing in his path.

"I praised God for making creatures that are varied. Different."

"Do you have brothers?" It turned out he had four—and three sisters.

"Are you the same as your brothers or different?"

He said proudly that his three brothers were short and stocky and brown-haired; he was taller and stronger and his beard was jet. "So when I see you," said Hannah Rochel, "I should say that same blessing for you? All your brothers and sisters and your parents should say it? The townspeople too, blessing you for being different?" A strange look fell on him. He stammered a soft apology for having given offense.

Hannah Rochel nodded, her eyes bright, satisfied.

On Chaim's seventh birthday, Hannah Rochel said how special the number seven was: seven branches of the sacred trees, seven days a baby kid must remain with its mother, seven offerings brought to the sanctuary, seven days of this and that holiday, and—and here she made a wide circular flourish with her arm—in the seventh year: the end of everything. Debts forgiven, slaves freed, the land left fallow for the widows, the orphans, the animals.

Meanwhile, Chaim danced in circles. Hannah Rochel asked, "You have other brothers, don't you?" I nodded. She blushed. "I met Nachshon years ago. He came into the factory store to buy . . . I don't know what. Could it have been cloth?"

I said it might have been cloth: the fabric for a suit my mother would sew, perhaps when he was leaving to attend the Yeshivah in Lublin. "He's a good student, too, isn't he?" She gave Chaim a playful push. "You, young man, take after your brother Nachshon."

"He's coming home for my birthday this Shabbos. At least I think so."

I laid fresh sheets for Nachshon that Friday in a corner of the room where Chaim and David and I slept. Although we set a place at the table and Chaim stayed awake until nearly midnight in anticipation, Nachshon didn't come home. He appeared at Chaim's birthday celebration after

Shabbos, bringing sweets, but he didn't stay with us. Instead Nachshon boarded in the home of Monesh Verbermacher, who had hired him to tutor Hannah Rochel. Turned out, it wasn't the first time. Turned out that despite the watchful eye of Mirla Verbermacher, Hannah Rochel and Nachshon had fallen in love. Turned out that Hannah Rochel loved him beyond reason. What did that even mean?

My mother was thrilled with the match. She had helped bring Hannah Rochel into the world—and here she was, a brilliant girl, about to marry Nachshon. "The Chernobyl rebbe foretold this," my mother said. "He required it: that the child be taught Torah and Talmud." But even the rebbe didn't predict that the child would excel not only in Hebrew studies, but in her father's business. Monesh's fellow tradesmen were astonished when he summoned her to go over details of a transaction or advise about a trade dispute.

My father continued to disapprove of Hannah Rochel–not her business savvy, which didn't concern him, but her assumption of a male role in her worship, her reading forbidden texts, her fearless bright-eyed challenges to the rebbes. He knew she was smarter than his own Nachshon, and wondered what would happen when she—not to mention, Nachshon—came to realize this. I was sure they both already knew.

Still, he did not stand in the way of the marriage. Sometimes on my way home from the market on a Wednesday afternoon, laden with sacks of onions and potatoes, I saw my father on the street at a time when he would usually be in the study house or the Cheder, tutoring or studying or praying. There he stood, in his worn coat and leather cap: his unmistakable curly red hair and beard, his slim erect posture, his pride. The factory of Monesh Verbermacher, Nachshon's future father-in-law, took up the entire block opposite where he stood. My father gazed at the building, oblivious to the folks (including me) walking past, with the same awe others showed only for the Chernobyl rebbe.

Meanwhile, my mother, when not attending to her midwife duties, began to spend time with Mirla Verbermacher. They had a warm relationship before but now she would say to me, *don't forget* Chaim's dinner or David's mush. *Don't forget* to take in the laundry, or scour the floors for Shabbos. *Don't forget* when you bake the challah to brush on the egg yolk so it shines—tasks that before she shared with me or did on her own. *Don't forget, don't forget, don't forget.*

I began to feel jealous of the amount of time my mother spent at Hannah Rochel's house. After returning from my walks with Hannah Rochel, before turning to my chores, I would take out my prayerbook or the Yiddish version of Bible stories, which is all I had to read. All I *could* read. I tried to be alert to the insights that flowed from Hannah Rochel, determined to find meanings that weren't obvious, that were below the surface, to share with her. But they remained simple stories to me.

When her engagement to Nachshon was announced, instead of happiness, I felt only loss. A married woman is part of her husband. Would Hannah ever be as open and friendly with me again? My brother Nachshon was a scholar. I knew he loved me, but he certainly didn't consider me his equal. And why should he? I never thought of myself as Hannah Rochel's equal and yet she treated me as if I were.

Evil thoughts assailed me. Until Chaim's birthday, until the engagement was announced, until the match was known throughout Volodymyr-Volynsky—to be celebrated or deplored—Hannah Rochel barely mentioned Nachshon on our walks. Suppose her friendship with me was intended to improve her chances with Nachshon? My head told me this was nonsense, but this thought took root in my chest and wouldn't let go.

I was on the verge of disappearing. My mother was absent and my father disapproved of my only real friend. As for my friend, I wondered if she loved me for my self—crippled, awkward and freckled, with a lazy eye and with no intellectual gifts—or for my brother's sake.

We continued our walks, to the meadows that bordered the town or along the river to the West. Sometimes Chaim studied with our father after Cheder, or went home with his study partner. Had I not had Hannah Rochel, I would have churned with envy: that my brother half my age had a friend and I had none. But his absence was a gift; without Chaim, it was just the two of us. Still, I brooded. Since her engagement, Hannah Rochel was distracted and dreamy. She smiled or laughed at nothing; crossed her arms in front of her body and hugged herself; rubbed her back in the tall grass when we sat by the river, like a dog with fleas. She threw pebbles ceaselessly into the panting current, marveling at the ever-expanding circles.

I dropped pebbles in the river too, but they barely dented the surface. I quoted Psalm 39, hoping to impress her even as I gathered my courage: "I kept silent; but had no peace, no comfort."

She looked at me intently, silently waiting, her eyes open but calm.

"I must ask you," I said. Her serenity inviolate. Later her followers would come to know that look, *say what you will, I'm here*, but at that moment, it was all mine.

"Why didn't you tell me about Nachshon? He's my brother. I only learned of it from gossip. I thought, it can't be true. Hannah Rochel would have said something. It's a mistake."

"I am so sorry. Until it happened, I didn't believe it would." Now the pebbles drifted through her splayed fingers. "I was afraid you would tell your mother, who would tell your father, who would send Nachshon away. Not simply back to Lublin, but further away, to Kremenetz, or Chernobyl." She looked troubled. I regretted causing her pain.

Then my mother was never home and we came to know the reason. Mirla Verbermacher was ill. It was a woman's illness or at least Mirla thought so which is why she summoned my mother instead of the one Jewish physician in Volodymyr-Volynsky, who treated patients in the neighboring towns as well. Some people worried that this doctor, Dr. Rhys, brought disease from town to town and house to house but my mother said that was a lie.

One day Hannah Rochel wasn't at Cheder anymore. I went to meet Chaim and we walked home in silence. I asked what he had learned but he said, "nothing much. Hannah Rochel wasn't there."

Days and nights passed. My mother was gone most of the time. I wanted to go with her to the Verbermacher house but she said she needed me at home. I had twice as much housework and child-care duty; it became a chore even to get Chaim to go to school. One day my mother came home past midnight. I heard her heavy footstep, rose from bed, drew a shawl around my shoulders. I hoped for a word about Hannah Rochel. My mother, her grey hair awry, her face wet and exhausted said. "Adonai Natan, Adonai Lakach, Yihee Shem Adonai Mivorach." *God gives, God takes away, blessed be the Name of God.*

It was several terrible minutes before I realized it was Mirla Verbermacher who had died and not Hannah Rochel.

I saw Hannah Rochel in the house of mourning. Nachshon was there, hovering over her or sequestered with the men while the women sat together and keened. She looked at me, her eyes heavy with tears, and turned back to her prayers. She prayed in a simple garment, which was torn, as is customary for mourners. She looked like any other mourning daughter; mourners are forbidden to wear tefillin, since it is considered an adornment, like finery.

After several weeks, she resumed her study and her teaching. But the joy had gone out of her voice and her step; more often than not, when I picked Chaim up from school, she would greet me but then head in the opposite direction. The Jewish cemetery was on the outskirts of town; sometimes I thought of accompanying her but usually I had to get Chaim home, get my work done. Would she even want the company? Meanwhile her wedding to Nachshon approached the following month. All of Volodymyr-Volynsky held their breath.

It snowed. Our breath danced before our faces.

We resumed our walks and made our way to the river. Hannah Rochel wore galoshes, her step again springy and lithe. I was in heavy boots, hand-me-downs from Nachshon. Hannah Rochel's cheeks were ruddy with cold; snow glistened in her hair, on her eyelashes; her eyes shone more brightly than they had since her mother died. We went slowly because of my leg; sometimes she seized my hands to help me over a snowbank. At the river, she spread out a heavy tarp. The river churned, dotted with ice floes. She leaned back in the snow, spread her arms, and waved her arms like wings, same as she did when it was a springtime meadow, covered in yellow flowers, wrapped in a violet haze. I told her she was making a snow angel, like Chaim did with his new friend from Cheder. She said, "You are right!" She told me that a medieval rabbi, a mystic, would lie down in the snow and flail his arms to rid himself of evil desires. "I think Rav Ezekiel invented the snow angel," she said in a mischievous tone.

Then she got serious. "It's a way to control one's feelings," she said, "when you don't want to have them. Or when you're not ready for them. All feelings are good or at least all feelings should be acknowledged. If they come from the heart."

"Does it work?"

"I'm not sure." She was happy, closed her eyes. The sadness from her mother's death had abated. I knew she was thinking of my brother, Nachshon, which made me feel strange. I did not want to think of her as Nachshon's mate.

She would become my sister so why was I so certain I would lose her?

One day, less than a week before her wedding, she wasn't at Cheder. Chaim was glum, toeing the dirt with his shoe. "Something happened to Hannah Rochel," he said. "Something happened." We raced home—me at an ugly half-gallop, my foot dragging in the dust—to see what my mother might know. She wasn't there.

Days later, I would learn: How Hannah Rochel became fixed on visiting her mother's grave after the evening prayers. How she felt the need to seek anew her mother's blessing of the forthcoming marriage. How she strode along the back streets, a shawl covering her head and shoulders, the hem of her skirt clogged with mud.

The gate to the cemetery was closed and locked, but there was a gap on one side and Hannah Rochel was slender enough to slip through. A heavy curtain of clouds shrouded everything in darkness. No matter. She knew the path to the grave without a lamp, without even a candle. She sank to her knees.

"Ima," she said, "I'm here." That's when the sky lit up.

That bright sky was the last thing Hannah Rochel remembered. Someone found her lying beside her mother's grave. Someone brought her home. Someone (my mother, it turned out, whom they called first) removed Hannah Rochel's muddy dress, her heavy boots. Someone eased her into a white nightgown, like a bride might wear, but in this case, almost like a shroud.

During that week, I tried to stay awake until my mother returned home at night so I could learn about the progress of Hannah Rochel's illness. For surely it was an illness, although no one knew quite what to call it. "Can she hear us?" Monesh asked daily, when they discussed her condition in grave voices. Every morning, my mother rushed out of our house. "Is she still with us?" she'd ask when she arrived. Only once did she let me come along. I persuaded her that, because of our friendship, my presence, even my voice, might help Hannah Rochel. My slow pace as we climbed the hill to Hannah Rochel's home frustrated my mother. I did my best, whispering urgently to my lame right leg to hurry.

Finally, we arrived. "Is she still with us?" my mother asked.

Then we were in her room. Hannah Rochel had always been beautiful in her distinctive boyish way, warm and inviting, but now her pallor made her appear remote. I reached out and touched her cheek before anyone could stop me. It was cool but not cold and when I murmured "Hannah Rochel" I could swear her eyelashes fluttered. But I found myself miserable with desperation; my wanting to save her was too intense; my own body's heat engulfed me. When the doctor arrived and complained about too many people in the room, I left without protest.

The following day was the sixth day. And when the sixth day turned to night, her eyes opened. When she saw her father's weary and worried face above her, saw behind him my mother, and saw behind her Dr. Rhys, Hannah Rochel leaned forward. She tried to sit up. Someone put a pillow behind her; someone else brought a cup of water to her lips. She smiled at them all. It took a full minute for her to form words.

"I have been to the heavenly court. And there they gave me a new and lofty soul."

The wedding was off. Hannah Rochel refused to go through with it. Nachshon moved back to Lublin. My father was relieved, but also felt the sting of humiliation on Nachshon's behalf; my mother was sad and perplexed.

As for me, I would be lying if I didn't say I experienced a new sensation, for me: hope.

The hope was short-lived. Hannah Rochel's conduct was condemned. She had shamed a Jewish boy; Monesh was guilty since he was responsible for his daughter's contracts. My father, against my mother's wishes, brought a complaint before a rabbinic court. The judge ordered Monesh to pay a fine and return all presents Hannah Rochel or her family had received, including—it was said—a gold pocket watch and a silver cigarette box. There were no such gifts, at least not from Nachshon.

Some say Hannah Rochel's refusal to marry Nachshon killed Monesh. He died seven months later, having become—among the property owners of Volodymyr-Volynsky—as much of a pariah as Hannah Rochel. They were no longer allowed to pray in either of the two synagogues in town; she was no longer welcome at Cheder. Only his business didn't suffer; his tradespeople were from towns that mostly didn't care about our scandal. They were dealing with the new taxes and restrictions on Jews imposed by Tsar Alexander. Monesh was gone from Volodymyr-Volynsky more and more; sometimes Hannah Rochel went with him. Finally, she returned and he stayed.

My parents forbade me any contact with this haughty young woman who had shamed us all.

I wanted to see her. I became convinced that my jealousy of Hannah Rochel's impending marriage caused her descent into illness, that my unspoken emotional turmoil led her to reject Nachshon. I would awaken at 4:30 or 5 a.m., my heart pounding, sure that I was responsible, the ordinary ache in my right leg replaced by acute restlessness in both limbs. My lazy eye blinked and began to itch uncontrollably, seeing shapes in the dark. I would rise from my bed, splash icy water on my face, dress, and slip out. I would make my way slowly, laboriously, through streets that were not yet noisy and alive. By the time I arrived at the Jewish cemetery, it was light and the gates were open: to mourners, to women who chanted Modeh Ani by the graves of their mothers, to the gravediggers pounding a patch of earth, preparing for a new tenant. I soon found the grave of Hannah Rochel's mother. I hoped to find Hannah Rochel there. But my timing was always off; I never did. Instead, I would leave a small stone on the grave marker, laying it gently beside the stones already aligned in tribute. I imagined that when Hannah Rochel arrived later that day, she would sink once more to her knees, notice the extra stone—for she noticed everything—and know who had placed it there.

When word came that Monesh had died, even those who scorned father and daughter felt sorry for her. People said she was crazy; that she hadn't been in her right mind all along. Now they had an excuse to go inside her grand house again. So did I. The mirrors were covered with black cloth but now a layer of dust covered everything. There were fewer people to offer comfort. I helped Hannah Rochel clean when the visitors left. I could see the room where she studied and prayed, piled high with books and scrolls.

It would be over a month before she came by our modest ground floor flat, the three rooms I shared with my parents and my brothers. Unlike her house on Farna Street, our little rooms shone, clean and sparsely furnished. I was mindful that others in town fared much worse. Only a few, like the Verbermachers, had large brick houses of generous proportions. When her parents were alive, they had servants, a luxury I could not even imagine. But now the only servant was the elderly maidservant who had accompanied Mirla to visit the seer of Chernobyl, the rebbe who prophesied her birth. Hannah Rochel showed up at our flat without warning. Somehow, she knew only I would be there. She proudly unfurled the deed to the brick building on Sokalska Street, where she would establish a Beit Midrash.

In a matter of weeks she sold the house on Farna Street and moved into the small rooms on the third floor of the Sokalska property. The second floor was for her Beit Midrash. On the ground floor the sexton lived in one room and the elderly maidservant in the other.

Thus began the six-year reign of Hannah Rochel and her followers, who came to be called—much to the consternation of the illustrious rebbes of Volhynia—the *Hasidim of the Moyd of Ludmir.* Ludmir was the Yiddish name of Volodymyr-Volynsky. On Shabbos mornings, the street in front of the building was crowded with women of all ages and backgrounds, some dressed in fine clothes, others in rags. Some men joined them too. By the end of the day, when all had left, after listening and praying and eating, the rug in the entrance was always filthy with mud and grit and dust and crumbs and would need to be cleaned for the next onslaught.

Defying my parents, I became one of her most faithful followers. When the service and afternoon Tish was over, when everyone else had left, I would stay and clean alongside the old servant and Hannah Rochel. Hannah Rochel's cleaning was half-hearted, her mind and spirit elsewhere. But it gave me the chance to spend time with her. Even the silence was precious to me. For when her anteroom was filled, the wave of people brought their individual auras and voices and peculiarities. The crowd jostled and strained to see and hear her. During one service, a hoarse voice ordered me to move from my prize spot near the alcove where Hannah Rochel was half-hidden from view. "Please. You are in my way. My hearing is pfft! I must watch her lips." The speaker's own lips were wet, dotted with saliva. He sat in a wheelchair, white hair sprouting in unruly tufts, partly obscured by a black yarmulke. His suit was shiny from wear, old and tattered like the rest of him. An old man was a rarity in Hannah Rochel's Beit Midrash. Most of her followers were women or young, destitute men, menial workers who couldn't afford the tributes demanded by the Hasidic rebbes. The Moyd never asked for a kopeck; she would reject it if it were offered. Instead, she gave: amulets of green jasper for physical healing, striped agate to those in mental torment, food on Shabbos afternoons. They flocked to her, calling her, familiarly, *the Moyd*—which simply meant *the maiden.* They listened to her Torah discussions, her pure voice singing hymns of praise—like a young boy's or an angel's. The ill and infirm lined up early, seeking a private moment: half obscured by a screen, her slender arm reached out to touch and heal an errant limb, a palsied cheek, an aching breast, an ear that wouldn't stop ringing. I was too much my mother's daughter to believe in magical healing power invested in any one person. Besides, Hannah Rochel was my friend; wouldn't she long ago have cured my lameness? Wouldn't she have strengthened my weak, wandering, overworked eye?

Her words of Torah usually explained part of the weekly portion. Years later, after I was engaged, if my groom-to-be mentioned a Parshah by name, I might say, well Hannah Rochel said such-and-such or pointed out such-and-such. He listened patiently.

I never thought of her as *the Moyd*, only as Hannah Rochel.

One day some boys flung mud at the windows of the building on Sokalska Street. When Hannah Rochel appeared in the window to investigate, stones flew. When she went to the open-air market, she was first ignored, then spat on. In the beginning, when she first established her Beit Midrash, her teaching and her debates and her stirring voice were a novelty. Now the town's Hasidic rebbes—and even the most illustrious rebbes in the neighboring towns—found themselves losing not simply arguments but adherents to the Moyd. It was one thing to lay tefillin; she could debate the local rebbe about that. Hadn't Michal, daughter of the biblical King Saul, wife of King David, worn tefillin too? But her assumption of the role of rebbe, the fact that she came to be called an Admor—a spiritual leader of Hasidim—this was unacceptable.

My involvement with Hannah Rochel led my parents to seek a match for me with new resolve. When I was 21 years old, they found one. I longed to tell Hannah Rochel about him, to get her blessing. But how to bring it up? Her mind was on spiritual matters.

Then one day she came again to our flat. She was bleeding, her clothing torn; a group of hoodlums had attacked her and run away screaming that she was possessed by a dybbuk, that she was a secret Christian, that they had seen her creeping in the night from the Uniate monastery in town, from the building where nuns lived. My mother tended to her. In spite of everything, I think my mother still cared for her. My engagement also made my mother feel more secure about my future, that it would not be ruined by my entanglement with Hannah Rochel.

After she dressed Hannah Rochel's bleeding face, my mother left us alone. Before she left, she said, "Tirzah has news for you, Hannah Rochel." She paused. "Good news."

I told Hannah Rochel that I was engaged, to an older widower, true, but one with raven-black hair and a high forehead. He had only one child, a son, the same age as Chaim. When we were introduced, I looked at him and said "you!" and he bowed his head and said, "I know! I am sorry. But oddly, after that day, I kept thinking of you. How happy you looked until I spoke and said that blessing. And how the Moyd—she wasn't the Moyd yet—chastised me. She was right. Even if difference is beautiful, even if it displays God's love of his creatures, it was wrong to point it out in that way." He looked into the distance. "Perhaps I can make it up to you."

"The man who walked away! Now he has come back to you." Hannah Rochel hugged me for the very first time. How delicate she was, with bones that felt as if they could break, but also surprisingly strong.

I had no idea why she had come, risking the animosity that awaited her on every other corner of Volodymyr-Volynsky; every other because in between there were people who loved her, who would swarm around her to touch her or merely to gaze on her blue-gray eyes, her shining cheeks. "I came here seeking your advice," she explained, "but perhaps this isn't the right time." The Moyd of Ludmir asking *me* for advice. She told me that the great seer of Chernobyl had come to see her. He arrived in a handsome carriage pulled by four high-stepping horses. His robes were velvet, deep blue. *Indigo*. This was the same sage who had prophesied her birth—or at least that is what he said. Now, he said, times had changed. She was no longer a feckless girl. It was time for her to marry, to live like other women. "What do you think?" I was stunned that she sought my counsel. I was to marry in several weeks. Wouldn't our marriages bring us closer in some way? Perhaps we would become pregnant at the same time. Would our friendship resume the way it was before Hannah Rochel became the Moyd?

Then she said, "Of course I would continue my Beit Midrash. The rebbe did not say I could not."

"Do you like him?" I asked.

"The groom? Well enough," she said. "He is my sexton. I see him every day."

I was one of a handful of female followers who sat with her in a room, while the groom, Moshe David, sat in another with his male friends and relatives. Hannah Rochel had refused an elaborate wedding but the traditional seven blessings were said. Then the bride and groom retreated to be alone. What happened next is unknown to all except them. Hannah Rochel has never shared it with me. Most of her followers said she remained pure on her wedding night; the groom's entourage said of course her husband fulfilled his obligations. But soon she had locked herself in the rooms above the Beit Midrash and sent a message to Moshe David seeking a divorce. After all, when she renounced her engagement to Nachshon, hadn't the rabbis said that a divorce was preferable to a broken engagement? Moshe David granted the divorce without complaint, without extracting any money or other recompense, almost (some would say) too easily.

Something had gone wrong. And it didn't end there.

The next Shabbos as I approached the Beit Midrash, I saw an old man hobbling down Sokalska street, tapping his cane in front of him, seeking solid ground. This was the same Hasid who showed up for the Moyd every Shabbos in his wheelchair, who insisted on sitting in the front because of his poor hearing.

So why was he plodding away from the Beit Midrash, not towards it?

"Pfft! I am through with the Moyd. Her lips move but there is nothing for me. Perhaps," and now he leaned heavily on his cane, "perhaps she is a fraud."

A fraud? How could anyone could say that? But he was old and hard of hearing. I was late for shul. I told him I was impressed to see him walking. Where was his wheelchair? "I donated it to my rebbe in Lutsk. I stopped needing it soon after the Moyd took notice of me. But I liked it. It enabled me to be close to her. Even though my hearing improved, my walking improved, why change things? Now, though, I will go elsewhere. In Lutsk, the rebbe keeps the wheelchair on hand for whomever might need it. If I show up, he will give it to me, for sure."

What about the Moyd's direct relationship with the divine? Even though her marriage lasted but a day, in the eyes of the old man and dozens of her followers, her healing powers were diminished; when asked simple questions, she foundered. With the exception of a few loyal followers, many believed she was now simply a pious woman—no more and no less. Even her words of Torah no longer seemed inspired. Before, her teaching about the first chapter of Exodus was repeated with awe. "Moses asks God's name," she would begin. "And what was God's response?" She paused for emphasis. "Ehyeh asher ehyeh. *I will be what I will be.*" Her eyes and cheeks glowed. "I will be what I will be. Isn't that true of each of us as well?" Her voice reverberated in the anteroom; the crowd murmured their approval. Some of them wept. What *they* would be, or hoped to become, was healed in body, or healed in mind, or both—by Hannah Rochel.

After the disastrous marriage that lasted one day, everything was different. Now the Moyd's interpretation of "Ehyeh asher ehyeh," in which she compared God's ineffable existence to human frailty and change, was, at best, foolishness; at worst, blasphemy.

Except to me. Was I too enamored to see this falling off? Maybe. But I also viewed it as temporary. And the fickleness of her public the same. After my wedding, I worried about her feeling lonely. But then I remembered that she used to walk the meadows and along the river on her own before we took those walks together. She told me so. It was she who told me that a person's noble thoughts shield her from loneliness; and something else: that every moment of existence is for itself; all that we think and experience is no longer in the past but exists in the present, renewed and real to us.

The Biblical tale Hannah Rochel returned to most often was the one she discussed when I last heard her preach, the week before my wedding. *Jacob is completely alone*, she always began, *alone in the dark. All of us have been there, haven't we?* She told the story: With no warning, someone or something lunges for Jacob, wrestles him to the ground. He fights valiantly for hours. Only as dawn approaches does this divine creature or angel or figment of Jacob's imagination (Hannah Rochel never said that; that's my mother's doubting voice, inside me) manage to wrench Jacob's hip at its socket. The damage done, his assailant turns to leave—but Jacob won't let it go.

"First, you must bless me!" Really? Why does Jacob seek a blessing from a being that caused him harm, that made him lame? Every time Hannah Rochel taught this portion, I thought she would explain it to me.

She never did. Perhaps that is its meaning: I will have to figure it out myself.

For Hannah Rochel, Jacob's ordeal surely means something different. After the battle is over, before he limps away, Jacob names the place where the two wrestled. He calls it *Peniel*, meaning, "I have seen a divine being face to face, yet my life has been preserved." Was that how Hannah Rochel thought about her vision at her mother's grave?

Someday soon I will ask her.

The Maiden of Ludmir: A Jewish Holy Woman and Her World by Nathaniel Deutsch and *Jewish Ludmir: The History and Tragedy of the Jewish Community of Volodymyr-Volynsky* by Volodymyr Muzychenko, translated from the Ukrainian by Marta Daria Olynyk, provided historical background for this story.

Joy Moore

This Other Life

Emptied of anything it held
before—a glass, a package, a half-case of cans—
the black plastic liquor store bag
guzzled wind and went drinkless and tipsy-turvy
across the park's arboretum, a high-
soaring stringless kite. I watched it fly by loblolly
pines and black oaks, over saucer
magnolias, past the dawn redwood and cedar, where
it settled to rest near gingkos.
For years, mine had been the vodka of volume, call it
top-shelf involvement, until a friend told me,
Sober up in stillness. So I'd set it all aside that day,
to see how quiet quiet is. In the park,
I ran my hand along the persimmon's pyramid-ridged
bark, spun a fallen redwood twig
between my fingers, its tiny copper gladiola of cone buds.
Studied tree names, considered
their sheddings, their shapes. And felt a wind catch
something loose in me, snap it taut,
and sail me, wind-filled where I'd never known was not.

Originally published in 32 Poems

David Naimon

May Your Memory Be a Blessing

Remember

the before?

Member

You must remain offshore, on your boat, for 40 days before you can come ashore. You must stay apart from us in a confined space, for a *quarantino*, a span of 40 days.

Mem

The Hebrew letter *mem* is a confined space with a narrow entrance/exit, often thought of as representing a womb. Its numerical value is 40, for the 40 weeks of gestation, the quarantino of the bambino.

Em

Em, the word for mother.

M

Mayim, the word for water, begins and ends, like the stern and bow of a boat, with the letter *mem*, the letter most associated with water.

Mem

Mysteriously, water existed before the world was created. God hovered over it like a wind in darkness. It was from this undifferentiated watery darkness, the *tovu vavohu*, that YHWH spoke the world into being.

Member

But God also destroyed the earth with water. Noah spent 40 days and 40 nights confined to a boat before it was safe to come ashore.

Remember

The billionaires who buy bolthole homes in New Zealand to ride out the apocalypse.

The headline *"European Union condemns rescue boats picking up drowning refugees"*

Óscar Alberto Martínez Ramírez & Angie Valeria

The *White Lion*

Member

The Black Death was the deadliest pandemic ever, which, at its peak, reduced the population of Europe by half and the world population from 450 million to 350 million. More en vogue to fight the plague than quarantine was the extermination of Jews. The Erfurt massacre, the Basel Massacre, the Aragon massacre, the Toulon massacre, the Flanders massacre. 510 Jewish communities were destroyed for the "health" of Europe. In Strasbourg alone, 2000 Jews were burned alive on a single day, St. Valentine's Day. Purportedly a preventative measure (the plague had yet to reach the city), the ashes of Jews were nevertheless sifted through as they smoldered. By Christian residents eager to acquire new things.

Em

Em, the word for mother. *Emet*, the word for truth. *Met*, the word for death.

Truth, *emet*, comes from mother, comes from death.

Mem

Once in Egypt, long ago, Jews sheltered at home with lamb's blood on their doorposts and lamb's blood on their lintels waiting for the Angel of Death to pass over them and pass them over. The word for Egypt, *mitzrayim*, means "narrow place" and begins and ends, like water, with the nearly closed womb-like confined space of the letter *mem*, the womb from which a people will be born, a people that will roam for 40 years and cross two waters before they can be born.

Remem

Often described as an act of ritual purification by water, immersion in a mikveh does not cleanse you. Instead it changes your status and marks that change. Part of a mikveh is a *bor* or pit that contains 40 sa'ah of natural rain water. This 40 is not, or not just, the 40 of birth, of creation, but rather its opposite. According to Jewish tradition if something is mixed with twice its volume, it is considered nullified. The largest human is 20 sa'ah in volume, thus 40 sa'ah will nullify the self of the person immersed, will cause them to ask "what am I?"

Member

The mikveh is both a womb and a tomb, a place of creation, for water existed before the creation, for we came from water, for we are made of it (and for 40 weeks we could breathe it) and also, at the same time, a place of non-existence, a place we can no longer survive in, for water existed before the creation, for we came from water, for we are made of it, and yet cannot stay within it any longer. But perhaps returning briefly to that untenable space before we existed, from which we are made, the nullification of 40, of two 20s, perhaps holding us in that (de)generative space of (non)being, being held in it, tells us something.

Remember

The year 2020. A year of perfect vision, where everything we were was crystal clear. A plague year. An election year. A year of two 20s that marks a change in status. A year of two 20s that nullifies the self. A rebirth/debirth year. The Hebrew years 5780 and 5781.

Ember

Every year in Jewish mysticism Jews draw meaning

from the numerologic correspondence between the year to come and Torah verses whose letters match the year numerologically. 5781 is unusual in that there is not even one verse in all of the Torah with the numerical value of 5781. There is nowhere in the scroll, nothing that has been written or sung, to draw wisdom from to prepare for the year ahead.

Mem

In Tarot, the card corresponding to *mem* is The Hanged Man. This card corresponds to the element of water. It signals the breaking of patterns, metamorphosis, a change in status. This upside-down man represents suspension, like the immersed breathless person in a mikveh, who in that brief moment when not touching any of its sides or the bottom, suspended, in a womb, in a tomb, says a prayer to each of the four directions.

Em

Did water exist before God? Em.

Member

If we quarantine to avoid the Angel of Death, and quarantine, immersed, suspended in 40, to become, for a moment, death…what do we remember?

Remember

What we don't remember is like the escape goat. The

goat that was not offered to God as a sacrifice by the High Priest at the Temple of Jerusalem on Yom Kippur, but the other goat, the scapegoat who became the carrier of the sins of the community and was driven out into the desert. When Jesus fasted in the desert for 40 days and 40 nights (like Elijah and like Moses before him, each themselves fasting for 40 desert days and 40 desert nights), did the devil who tempted him appear in the form of a goat?

Member

Who is the devil? William of Norwich, Little Saint Hugh of Lincoln, Simon of Trent, Gabriel of Bialystok—we remember their names, innocents whose deaths were venerated, commemorated by feast days, sanctified, because they were killed by Jews. For their blood. They supplied a crucial ingredient in satanic (Jewish) Passover matzahs. Do you remember the names of the scapegoated?

     ____

& ____________

& ____________

& ____________

Ember

For centuries countless cats were killed by Christians because cats too were considered close to Satan and thus the carriers of disease. Without cats, the rat population, the actual vector of plague, grew unchecked. The more cats they killed the greater the Black Death became. The greater the Black Death became the more they hated cats. In what form does the devil appear?

Mem

That that desert was once an ocean.

Em

That that which we could once breathe.

M

is for mask. For we could once breathe water, for we could once breathe a plague-less air. The word for breath and the word for spirit and the word for wind are the same word. YHWH hovered over the watery darkness like a spirit or a wind or a breath.

Em

For as the days of a tree shall be the days of My people. No tree, no breath. No breath, no spirit.

Mem

The Hebrew words for mask, *masecha* & *masveh*, each begin with a *mem*.

Remember

Moses, *Moshe*, means "to be drawn from water." And *Moshe* begins with the letter of water. And *Moshe* spends 40 days, the number of the letter of water, away from the people, with YHWH. When he descends the mountain his face is so radiant from speaking with God that he must wear a mask.

Member

The most famous depiction of Moses, that of Michelangelo, depicts the prophet with horns like a goat, much as Moses' fellow Jews in the Middle Ages were often thought to have them, even forced to wear horned headdresses to demarcate themselves as Jews. But the horned Moses may be a result of a mistranslation from the Hebrew to the Latin. The Hebrew words for *horn* and *shining ray of light* were close and often interchanged. Moses spoke to God after 40 days and his face had become glorified, had become radiant, had become horned. He would never be the same, could never relate to others as an ordinary man again.

Ember

When Jesus fasted in the desert for 40 days and 40 nights, did the devil he encounter have a glorified face?

Remem

We must return a second time to this story of the boy "who was drawn from water" for it is not simple. But *strange.* A return to it will only make it stranger, doubly so.

Mem

What happens on the mountain where the boy who was drawn from water quarantines for 40 days and 40 nights before meeting God face to face? And why, unlike Noah, Elijah & Jesus, does Moses have to do this twice? Was the Mt. Sinai double *quarantino* both a womb and a tomb, a drinking and a drowning?

Remem

Moses, far up the mountain, gone away—unseen, unheard—for so so long, the people at the foot of the mountain desire a proxy, something tangible, physical, visible, and *there* to celebrate and worship. Aaron instructs them to melt down their gold to make a molten god, an *egel masecha.* But the word we translate as "molten," from the root "to pour in," is the same word we now use for "mask."

Mem

After 40 days without food and without water, Moses, the boy drawn from water, receives the covenant of God. Mt. Sinai is illuminated with this encounter, a glow that does not frighten the people below. But when Moses descends and sees his people worshipping a molten god, a mere mask, he breaks the tablets in anger.

Remem

A second time Moses refrains from food & water for another 40 days and another 40 nights. A second time Moses ascends the mount. A second time he receives a covenant from God, who in giving it, gives the people a second chance. But this time it is not the mountain that is radiant, horned, and glorified. It is Moses' face, a face so transformed from this second face to face with God, that it frightens the people. But why are they frightened now, by an illumination quite like the one that had horned Sinai, that they had welcomed before? Was it shame, the memory of having mistaken the mask for the masked? Either way, Moses forevermore, for the rest of his lived days, covered his face when among the people, hid his new face, to keep their uneasiness at bay.

Mem

Some say the reason Moses' face was glorified, not by his first encounter with God, but by his second, was to (re) assure the people that the second covenant was indeed a true covenant as well. Some say the first covenant came from the Tree of Life, the second covenant from the Tree of Knowledge of Good and Evil. That the first "before the Fall" covenant was Edenic, where humans were (and would've been again?) in harmony with the non-human other, where there was no shame in their nakedness, no killing needed to eat, no pain in the labor of birth, no labor needed to be fed from the earth. The "after the Fall" covenant, given after they fell again, was given to a people lost in the human forebrain of representation, as if that representation, that mask, were the thing itself, that molten god God.

Remem

For as the days of a tree shall be the days of My people.

Mem

is for *masveh.* Moses wore a *masveh*, a mask or veil, but a mask or veil referred to as a *masveh.* This is the only time this word, *masveh*, is used in the Torah. This is not a *masecha*, a molten god, a representation of God held before his face, but a woven fabric. The *masveh* was not a false representation. But it hid something true.

Remem

We return to Sinai a second time, a second ascent, a second fast, a second encounter, a second covenant, a second descent, and yet…

Mem

If two 20s, the volume of two human beings, 20 sa'ah twice, creates self-nullification, what do two 40s create?

Remem

The word for heaven in Hebrew, *shamayim*, means "double waters" or "second waters." Yet the word *mayim* itself, the word for water, is already in its plural form. Plural, just like the word *punim* for face, which is multiple too. What if we should be looking, not up into the heavens, into the double waters, the *shamayim*, not raising our heads, our faces, as *the boy drawn from water* ascends up high? What if we are looking in the wrong place? What if we have been looking at the wrong water with the wrong face?

Remember

Remember Miriam, way down below, at the foot of the mount, in the mount's shadow? Miriam whose name means "strong waters" and "bitter sea," Miriam who is not only or mainly Moses' sister, but a prophet, the same Miriam without whom the people could not survive, the prophet whose wellspring of water miraculously accompanied her as her people moved throughout the desert? The Miriam who, when she died, the well died too, and the people were thirsty. Miriam over whom the Angel of Death had no power. Miriam who died instead from a direct kiss from God. Miriam, one of the seven over whom the worms had no power. Miriam who wore no mask, who from the deep unseen and down below drew her strong waters. Was this prophet's face glorified too? Was her face radiant and horned, and no one stopped to notice? What if we allowed our faces to be plural, blessed both by the waters above and the waters below, if we saw ourselves in the faces of others, in the Uighurs forced to make our *masechas*, the Gazans denied vaccines or potable water in their open-air prison, the refugees fallen face down in a river of water that is a border? What if we remembered the escape goat and its song, our sins on its head, the home we denied it? What if we remembered when our lungs filled fully with the waters of another, our mother, when we lived in the womb, the tomb, the well, the ark, the garden, the darkness, the heavens?

Remember

the waters. Re-member the waters. The days of a tree. Remember when no one was a member, when all *punim* were sanctified and nullified, all faces radiant, glorified and horned. Re-*mem*-ber the before.

Originally published in EcoTheo Review

Darius Simpson

I Left the Church in Search of God

my momma is all knuckle no talk. hails from
northside akron front yard fights on carlysle. once

almost dragged a lady into the aldi's parkin lot over
ten cents. my mother is hard handed. but soft hearted

when it pays or keeps her children out harm's way.
she says *you are too smart to protest* with fists

unclenched. her voice stumbles soft and clumsy through
the phone. i am the youngest of three. her last dime

saved. when she pleads *stay home boy* i understand
she's frightened by memories of her baby nursing

his wrists scraped bloody by zip ties. or being taken
for a rough ride in a city she's never heard of.

she knows i'm quick to anger and means to uncurl my
reactionary fits. before a pig decides my pulsing

neck vein is a concealed weapon. my mother is a devout
    christian.
all the church regulars know bobbi best by ad libs. Recognize

the instigation of her *amen!* her *come on pastor!*
her *take ya time!* once inspired a bishop to keep

us in service for two days straight. she made sure i could

recite books
of the bible in my sleep hanging upside down. the first time
i'm arrested

at a protest she says my brain is better used in service of the lord's
work. she believes my voice is most effective as a sanctuary echo.

i wanna tell her about the morning i survived an armored truck
big as a chapel plowing through a residential neighborhood.
how i

know god is real because once after curfew i was cornered by
a squad
of headlights and i grew wings. flapped once and feathered home.

she says her biggest regret is not being the kind of person
who protests. and i wanna tell her how i scan the crowd

for the loudest person in attendance. and i find my mother
in the front row swaying near the megaphone. a sacred pulpit.

where a black woman who smiles just like her. screams holy
with her diaphragm turned skyward. how it feels like praise and

politics. how we sing *no justice!* and it sounds like
sunday mourning. i want to ask what good is the lord's work

if not demanding a piece of heaven on earth for all her children.
what use is my salvation if i can't pray with my feet first. if i
won't

stand ten toes against military cowardice. if i won't risk
whatever life i got left. if she could see us dance in the
intersection

we gon be alright electrifying each breath while we pass half
empty
water bottles like communion. arms woven like a thorn crown.
Guilty

and ready to accept the consequences. i think she'd bow her
head. say *praise god* thankful i found my church home.

Originally published in Southern Humanities Review

Gideon Young

kwansaba crown

this country says you were born flying
in the face of its oldest rule—
brown and loved. we lift you up
cradle your warm face to our faces
the murmur and spark of your skin
your blood crossed over ocean and swung
the lash. your wings gold and fire

...

lash your wings with gold and fire
invent fine knots that have no names
tie them snug around your green bones
this world wants to watch you fray
won't warn you the term for loop
is *eye.* an eye that slips is
called *noose.* you keep you in view

...

our name anew, keep you in view
pray the spirits of our spiral cells
their hope tall drums' tight deep boom
battle dance of spun blood toward light
each jitter red drop an elder's eye
under your skin their buzz a blue
ancient chorus hums power in your moves

...

ancient chorus hums power in your moves
i know from the clatter how elegant
your elbows bend to cast rainbow blocks
across our ash floors you unbuild towers
we made of selves before you sparked
your small fingers offer us bright bricks
more again, you say without saying, *here*

...

more again, you say without saying, here
watch me sway but stand toes curled
press my bones' weight into ash floors
yet of bones into ash into dust
i know nothing of winter except winter:
an absence of wild geese, early evening
sun on silver limbs, your lifted gaze

...

sun on silver limbs, your lifted gaze
burns away all of me but memory
how your skull above your ears fit
in the cradle of my spread fingers
your soft spot exact to the center
of my palm our pulse same rhythm
spring breeze charms the air with lilac

...

spring breeze charms the air with lilac
you ignore the grass between your toes
new word *more* a wren takes wing

out from the crayon in your fist
acorn filled with earth hear my yearn
my blood near yours forever i know
this world sings you were born flying

Originally published in North Carolina Literary Review

CONTRIBUTORS

Ser Álida is a Black Queer Dominican writer and educator. Her work dissects ideas of identity—blackness, queerness, womanhood, Dominicanidad, and language. As equity consultant for UnidosUS's Afro Latinx Lideres Avanzando Fellowship, she focuses on creating spaces where Black people can be and can reimagine their future. She is a 2021–2024 MFA Candidate in Fiction at the University of Mississippi.

Born to Pakistani-American immigrant artists, **Jai Hamid Bashir** was raised in the American West. She is the daughter of loomsmith, rug designer, and master weaver Hamid Bashir. With years of academic training, and a commitment to lifelong autodidactic learning, Jai studies various forms of mysticism and theology, climate justice, decolonization and subaltern literature, birth and death rites, gender and sexuality studies, psychoanalysis, animal studies, human and more-than-human systems, plant medicine, classical antiquity, land art, and other forms of inquiry and being. Bashir is a graduate of Columbia University MFA Program, where she was awarded the Linda Corrente Memorial Prize. She has also received an Academy of American Poets University Prize, The Zócalo Public Prize, and The 2020 Nostrovia! Prize.

Ellen Bass's most recent collection, *Indigo*, was published by Copper Canyon Press in 2020. Her other poetry books include *Like a Beggar*, *The Human Line*, and *Mules of Love*. Her poems appear frequently in *The New Yorker*, *American Poetry Review*, and many other journals. Among her awards are Fellowships from the Guggenheim Foundation, The NEA, and The California Arts Council, The Lambda Literary Award, and four Pushcart Prizes. She co-edited the first major anthology of women's poetry, *No More Masks!*, and her nonfiction books include the groundbreaking *The Courage to Heal: A Guide for Women Survivors of Child Sexual Abuse* and *Free Your Mind: The Book for Gay, Lesbian and Bisexual Youth*. A Chancellor of the Academy of American Poets, Bass founded poetry workshops at Salinas Valley State Prison and the Santa Cruz, California jails, and teaches in the MFA writing program at Pacific University.

Jack B. Bedell is Professor of English at Southeastern Louisiana University where he also edits *Louisiana Literature* and directs the Louisiana Literature Press. His work has appeared in *HAD*, *Bracken*, *Pidgeonholes*, *The Shore*, *Heavy Feather Review*, *Psaltery & Lyre*, *EcoTheo Review*, and other journals. His most recent collection is *Against the Woods' Dark Trunks* (Mercer University Press, 2022). He served as Louisiana Poet Laureate 2017–2019.

Wendy Cheng is the author of *The Changs Next Door to the Díazes: Remapping Race in Suburban California* (University of Minnesota Press, 2013) and the coauthor of *A People's*

Guide to Los Angeles (University of California Press, 2012). Her creative nonfiction has appeared or is forthcoming in *The Cincinnati Review*, *Boom California*, *Amerasia Journal*, *Tropics of Meta*, and *Brink*. She teaches American studies and ethnic studies at Scripps College and lives in Pasadena, California with her family.

Born and raised in Oregon, poet and author **Broderick Eaton** graduated from Sweet Briar College in Virginia. Motivated to publish following the passing of her mentor, Mary Oliver, her work has appeared in numerous publications. She is the recipient of the Sixfold Poetry Prize in addition to being named runner-up for the Erskine J. Poetry Prize and finalist for both the 49th Parallel Award and the poetry award in the Tucson Festival of Books. Her stories have been finalists for Sixfold and Tulip Tree Publishing contests. A poetry chapbook, *Black Bird Blue*, is forthcoming from Finishing Line Press in 2022. Eaton holds an MFA from Lindenwood University and lives with her family and an unreasonably large dog in the high desert of Oregon.

B. Tyler Lee is the author of the poetry chapbook *With Our Lungs in Our Hands* (Redbird Chapbooks, 2016). She won the 2020 Talking Writing Contest for creative nonfiction and participated in the Tin House '21 summer workshop. Her work has appeared or is forthcoming in *32 Poems*, *Crab Orchard Review*, *Hayden's Ferry Review*, *The Hunger*, *Jet Fuel Review*, *Whale Road Review*, and elsewhere. She lives with her children and partner in the Midwest.

Kenji C. Liu (劉謙司) is a writer, translator, and artist, author of *Monsters I Have Been* (Alice James Books, 2019), finalist for the 2020 California and Maine Book Awards for poetry, and *Map of an Onion*, national winner of the 2015 Hillary Gravendyk Poetry Prize. His work has appeared in numerous journals, anthologies, magazines, and two chapbooks, *Craters: A Field Guide* (2017) and *You Left Without Your Shoes* (2009). An alumnus of Kundiman, the Djerassi Resident Artist Program, and the Community of Writers, he lives in occupied Tongva land, Los Ángeles.

Nancy Ludmerer's fiction has appeared in *Kenyon Review*, *Electric Literature*, *Cimarron Review*, *New Orleans Review*, *Best Small Fictions* (a *River Styx* prizewinner), and *The Saturday Evening Post*. In recent years, her stories have won prizes from *Masters Review*, *Carve*, *Pulp Literature*, and *Streetlight*. Her short memoir "Kritios Boy" (*Literal Latte*) was named a notable essay in *Best American Essays*, and other nonfiction has appeared in *Green Mountains Review*, *The American Lawyer*, *Vogue*, and *Brain, Child*. She practiced law in NYC for many years and continues to live there with her husband Malcolm and recently-adopted 13-year-old cat Joseph.

Joy Moore lives in Tennessee, where for the last fifteen years she has taught undergraduate writing and interdisciplinary courses, designed and managed two coffee shops, and led a music and arts venue. Her poems have appeared in such journals as *32 Poems*, *Hunger Mountain*, *The Greensboro Review*, and *Prairie Schooner*, where she won The Glenna Luschei Award.

David Naimon is the host of the literary podcast Between the Covers (tinhouse.com/podcasts) and co-author, with Ursula K. Le Guin, of *Ursula K. Le Guin: Conversations on Writing*, a Hugo Award finalist and winner of The 2019 Locus Award in nonfiction. Naimon's writing can be found in *Orion*, *AGNI*, *Boulevard*, *Black Warrior Review*, *ZYZZYVA*, and elsewhere. It has received a Pushcart prize; been reprinted in *The Best Small Fictions*; and cited as notable in *Best American Mystery & Suspense*, *Best American Travel Writing*, and *Best American Essays*.

Darius Simpson is a writer, educator, performer, and skilled living room dancer from Akron, Ohio. Much like the means of production, he believes poetry belongs to and with the masses. He aims to inspire those chills that make you frown and slightly twist up ya face in approval. Darius believes in the dissolution of empire and the total liberation of Africans and all oppressed people by any means available. Free The People. Free The Land. Free All Political Prisoners.

Gideon Young is a member of the Carolina African American Writers' Collective with recent and forthcoming work in *Journal of Black Mountain College Studies*, *JUXTA*, *North Carolina Literary Review*, and *Our State Magazine*. His debut haiku collection, *my hands full of light*, was published by Backbone Press in 2021. Three chapter books for young readers, *Art for Change*, *Men Before Soldiers*, and *Prince Rivers: A Leader for Justice*, are forthcoming from Gibbs Smith in 2022 and 2023. Gideon is co-author of *One Window's Light: A Collection of Haiku*, published by Unicorn Press in 2017, winner of the Haiku Society of America Merit Award for Best Anthology. His film "A Curious Honeybee" was recently premiered by the Arts Education Partnership and the Education Commission of the States. Young is a Fellow for A+ Schools of North Carolina, a K-12 Literacy Specialist, and a stay-at-home dad.

ABOUT THE EDITORS

Luke Hankins is the founder and editor of Orison Books. He is the author of two full-length poetry collections, *Radiant Obstacles* and *Weak Devotions*, as well as a forthcoming chapbook, *Testament* (Texas Review Press, 2023). He is also the author of a collection of essays, *The Work of Creation*, and is the editor or co-editor of several anthologies, including *Poems of Devotion: An Anthology of Recent Poets* and *Between Paradise & Earth: Eve Poems* (with Nomi Stone). A volume of his translations from the French of Stella Vinitchi Radulescu, *A Cry in the Snow & Other Poems*, was published by Seagull Books in 2019.

Nathan Poole is the author of two books of fiction, *Father Brother Keeper* (Sarabande Books, 2015), a collection of stories selected by Edith Pearlman for the 2013 Mary McCarthy Prize and long-listed for the Frank O'Connor Award, and *Pathkiller as the Holy Ghost*, selected by Benjamin Percy as the winner of the 2014 *Quarterly West* Novella Contest. He has been awarded The *Narrative* Prize, a Milton Fellowship at *Image*, and a Joan Beebe Fellowship at Warren Wilson College.

Karen Tucker is the author of the novel *Bewilderness* (Catapult, 2021), which was selected as a "Dazzling Debut" by The American Booksellers Association and was longlisted for The Aspen Words Literary Prize and The Crook's Corner Book Prize. Tucker's short fiction can be found in *The Missouri Review*, *The Yale Review*, *Boulevard*, *EPOCH*, *Tin House*, and elsewhere. The recipient of an Elizabeth George Foundation Grant for Emerging Writers and a PEO Scholar Award, she teaches fiction and creative nonfiction at UNC Chapel Hill.

ACKNOWLEDGMENTS & PERMISSIONS

"Eulogy to a Tree" copyright © 2022 by Broderick Eaton.

"Love thy neighbor." copyright © 2021 by Ser Álida. Reprinted from *Southern Humanities Review* (#54.2) by permission of the author.

"The Apiarists" copyright © 2021 by Jai Hamid Bashir. Reprinted from *Tampa Review* (#61/62) by permission of the author.

"During the Pandemic I Listen to the July 26, 1965, Juan-les-Pins Recording of *A Love Supreme*" copyright © 2021 by Ellen Bass. Reprinted from *New England Review* (#32.2) by permission of the author.

"Ghost Forest" copyright © 2021 by Jack B. Bedell. Reprinted from *Psaltery & Lyre* (2021) by permission of the author.

"The Instant You Entered the Black Hole" copyright © 2021 by Wendy Cheng. Reprinted from *The Cincinnati Review* (#18.1) by permission of the author.

"And All God's Queer Girls Said *Amen*" copyright © 2022 by B. Tyler Lee.

"A Specter is Haunting Street View" copyright © 2021 by Kenji C. Liu. Reprinted from *Ecotone* (#30) by permission of the author.

"The Loneliness Cure" copyright © 2022 by Nancy Ludmerer.

"May Your Memory be a Blessing" copyright © 2021 by David Naimon. Reprinted from *EcoTheo Review* (Summer 2021) by permission of the author.

"This Other Life" copyright © 2021 by Joy Moore. Reprinted from *32 Poems* (#19.2) by permission of the author.

"I Left the Church in Search of God" copyright © 2021 by Darius

Simpson. Reprinted from *Southern Humanities Review* (#54.3) by permission of the author.

"kwansaba crown" copyright © 2021 by Gideon Young. Reprinted from *North Carolina Literary Review* (#30) by permission of the author.

ABOUT ORISON BOOKS

Orison Books is a 501(c)3 non-profit literary press focused on the life of the spirit from a broad and inclusive range of perspectives. We seek to publish books of exceptional poetry, fiction, and non-fiction from perspectives spanning the spectrum of spiritual and religious thought, ethnicity, gender identity, and sexual orientation.

As a non-profit literary press, Orison Books depends on the support of donors. To find out more about our mission and our books, or to make a donation, please visit www.orisonbooks.com.

For information about supporting upcoming Orison Books titles, please visit www.orisonbooks.com/donate, or write to Luke Hankins at editor@orisonbooks.com.

www.ingramcontent.com/pod-product-compliance
Lightning Source LLC
Chambersburg PA
CBHW031027190726
48286CB00003BA/1053

* 9 7 8 1 9 4 9 0 3 9 3 7 5 *